IMPRINT
CLASSICS

Our
Flying
Aces

ION IDRIESS

ETT IMPRINT
Exile Bay

First published in Imprint Classics by ETT Imprint 2025

Copyright © Idriess Enterprises Pty Ltd 2025
First edition hardback by ETT Imprint 2025

Transcribed and edited by Tom Thompson

ETT IMPRINT
PO Box R1906
Royal Exchange NSW 1225 Australia

ISBN 978-1-923205-89-5 (Limited First Edition of 50 only)

ISBN 978-1-922698-25-4 (paper)
ISBN 978-1-922698-26-1 (ebook)

Cover: Oswald Watt, with his aeroplane
'Advance Australia' on French soil.

Design by Tom Thompson

CONTENTS

FOREWORD

Tim Bowden

Ion 'Jack' Idriess remains one of Australia's finest story tellers and certainly one of the most prolific. His books are as Australian as billy tea and remain as refreshing to read as they were when first published in the early part of the twentieth century.

I was privileged to interview Idriess in 1975 for the ABC at his home on the cliffs of Mona Vale, Sydney. Idriess was then 86 (I am now 84!), and the transcript was preserved and now published as *The Last Interview* by ETT Imprint in 2020 – a publisher now specialising in the re-printing of all Idriess' amazing oevre.

In 2022, yet another of Idriess' manuscripts, *Our Flying Aces,* has been rediscovered profiling some of the remarkable pilots who flew their 'string and ceiling wax' aircraft fearlessly against the Germans in the World War I, not only bombing targets on the Western Front, but engaging in hair-raising aerial combat against German biplanes sent up to shoot them down. These are ripping yarns indeed profiling intrepid young Australians who risked their lives (and many were killed) in this war that was supposed to be the war to end all wars.

Lawrence Hargrave.

1

The Dreamer of the Skies

LAWRENCE Hargrave in 1866 was sixteen years of age, a dreamy, but restless boy. He wanted to do great things but he did not yet quite know what. In all this big world there must be something big for him to do. He determined to find out what it was. And do it.

In his wildest dreams he did not et imagine what that work was to be. Through his work, as with Lilienthal, Pilcher, and Chanute the flying machine was made possible. Men dream the maddest things. Often ridicule is heaped upon them, they have to grit their teeth in silence and toil against the scorn of the world. Of stern stuff indeed is the practical dreamer made.

Hargrave was destined to be the pioneer upon whose plans and experiments other men built aeroplanes. Willingly he gave his plans to the world.

But the restless boy of sixteen did not yet know this. The smell of the Bush was calling, the tang of distant seas. He lived in a pioneer country, a great continent in which the very air seemed to whisper a lad to be up and doing things.

His Dad wanted him to study Law. But Hargrave with Alick Thompson of Toowoomba sailed aboard the barque *Ellesmereon* an exploring voyage along the Gulf of Carpentaria. Here he heard the song of the Bullroarer, listened to the wild men chanting of love and the hunt and war in the wilds of Sweers and Bentinck islands, saw moonlight on the tropic sea, battled through the white squalls of the Strait. He loved the hard, adventurous life.

The wheeling gulls, the wild geese flying through night to the mainland, fascinated him. The plunge of the porpoise through the water, the swirl of the shark, the lazy swim of the dugong stirred dreams of movement through his mind. On return to Sydney Dad persuaded him to enter the drafting room of the engineering shops of the Australasian Steam Navigation Company. Here he learned a technical efficiency which was o prove of considerable value in the great work to come.

The New Guinea gold boom broke out, hectic tales of adventure and derring-do came floating to Sydney from that wild land. And young Hargrave listened eagerly again to the siren call of Adventure.

In a flurry of excitement the "New Guinea Prospecting Association" was formed to exploit golden New Guinea and open up trade with the natives.

Young Hargrave immediately joined the seventy-five adventurers who quickly banded together. A somewhat wild and woolly crowd they were all met in the spurt of adventure. With a laugh on their lips, eager plans all too hurriedly thought out.

They wanted to be up and doing and away. They bought the old brig *Maria,* a tub of 167 tons that for years had waddled the northern coast in the Newcastle coal trade. She could by no means be classed as seaworthy, neither was her skipper the best that sailed the seas but the high-spirited lads were perfectly satisfied and anxious to up-anchor and away to the "Isles of Gold."

The Authorities frowned upon the expedition, called them would-be filibusters and even worse. Trouble loomed ahead before the adventurers could slip away.

They cleared the Heads, to their wild delight. Bad weather came, big seas smashed over the clumsy craft, the tiller broke and they began drifting at the memory of the waves.

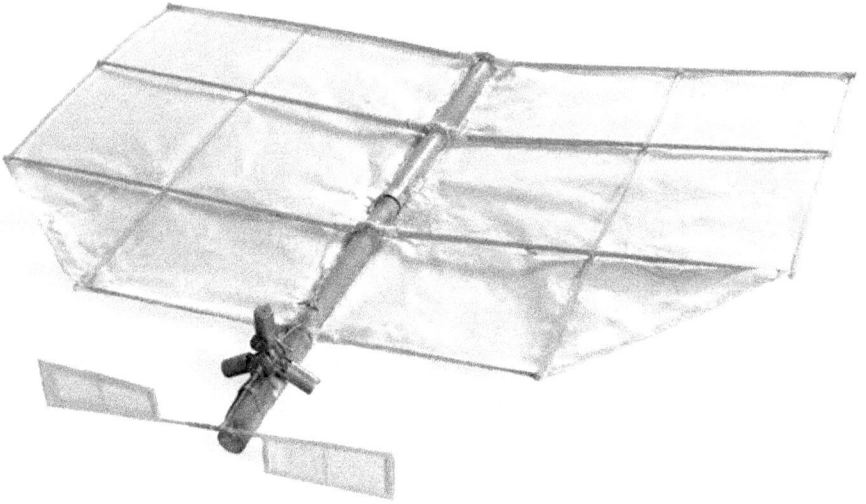

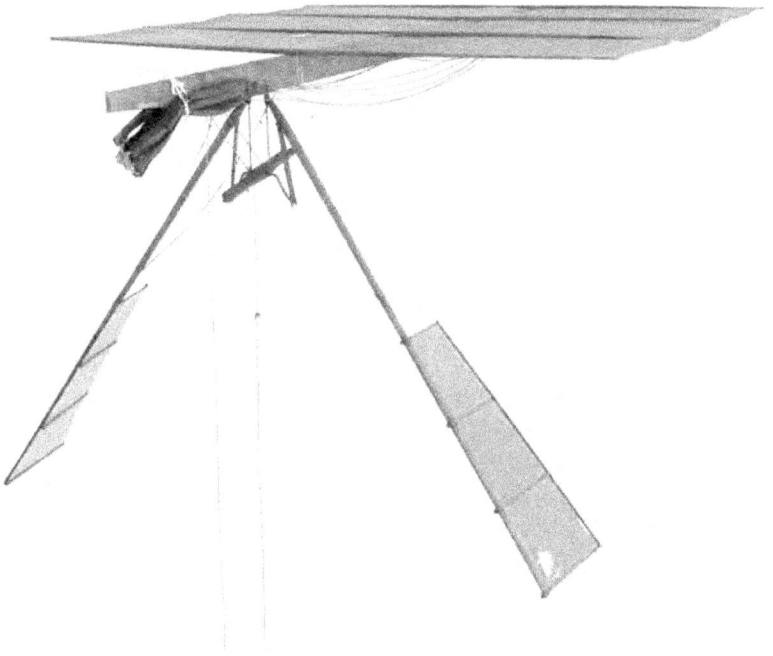

Hargrave's Flying Machine, 'Experiments', 1887. Both MAAS Collection.

"The end of the Golden Rainbow," laughed a manly lad. "It's Davey Jones locker for us now."

But young Hargrave hurriedly set to and mortised a capstan bar to replace the tiller. They "hurrahed!", regained control of the brig again and declared Hargrave a pukka engineer. They toasted him on the tiny deck and roared a joy song as the clumsy craft waddled on.

They crawled north up the Queensland coast and wondered that New Guinea could be so far away. If only they had first realized what really lay ahead of them.

They were just off Cardwell when thunder clouds came again, big seas rolled in from the Pacific, the *Maria* pitched and tossed and groaned in every cranky timber. A storm moaned in with a howl and driving mists that blotted out the world. The *Maria* was battered by mountainous seas, she bagan to break up, amongst the confusion of the seas and the confusion aboard came "Crash!" She struck on Bramble Reef, broken waves crashed down upon her, slowly she began to sink.

Those who could escaped in two boats while the others hurriedly built two rafts with the brig going down under them, timber by timber. Most of these men got away on the rafts and disappeared to suffer awful hardships. Others were drowned. Hargrave, with the brig going down, shinned up the topmast. One of the boats managed to pull alongside and took him off. By such a slender thread hung the life of the man destined to make possible the flying machine.

One boat reached Cardwell, one raft reached the mainland and the castaways were well treated by the blacks. But all the men on the raft were killed. The full story of the tragedy will take up too much space to tell here. H.M.S. *Baselisk* rescued the survivors, only forty of the seventy-five who had left Sydney with such high hopes. "Spirited but hair-brained young men from Sydney," Admiral Morseby termed them.

But Lawrence Hargrave was now a very tough lad, determined too. It took more than a shipwreck and hostile natives to stop him. He

Lawrence Hargrave with his flying machine at Stanwell Park in 1896.

Lawrence Hargrave experimenting with box-kites at Point Piper in 1910.

got to New Guinea in the *Chevert* with William Macleay's expedition to the Gulf of Papua. The *Chevert* was a barque of 314 tons, originally built as a French man-of-war of fourteen guns. Hargrave secured a job in charge of the steam launch. This launch was to be used by the expedition in steaming up unknown rivers.

Young Hargrave, during these exploring trips (he did six years of them) always worked his passage. But he was well content. Fascinated by the flights of the countless birds of many species, by the movements of their wings. Studying the countless queer movements of tides and currents and eddies among islands and reefs. Watching for hours, for days and weeks and months the movement of waves and how they reacted to winds and currents, tides and storms and calms. Wondering at the lifting powers of waves and the pressure of the atmosphere upon them. Watched the birds and found that they get lifting and flying power from the waves as the air is pushed up and falls down.

He would sit for hours watching the practice of a New Guinea warrior with bow and arrow, watching the flight of the arrow, its course and angle and distance travelled through the air. He mused on the propelling power of the bowstring. The tautening, then sudden relaxing of that bowstring meant power, cheap yet efficient power. It was the power that propelled the long arrow swiftly and true to a surprising distance away. And that arrow was heavier than the air into which it swiftly rose and flew. Mentally he was devising methods by which that arrow might be made to fly further and travel straighter. But it was not of an arrow he was thinking, he was thinking that it was possible to make a stick of wood fly through the air it must also be possible to make something much heavier rise and travel through the air. He watched and studied every moving thing he could see on land, in the air, under the ground, and in the sea. He wondered that a fish could fly, but Man could not.

He tried to understand the working of the physical mechanism which gave to each its particular power of movement. He even studied the movement of worms within the earth, and of worms crawling along the sea bottom.

Most intensely interested was he in the wing power of birds, the mechanism of long flight birds, short flight birds, diving birds, soaring birds, ground birds. He studied low down over the sea. He tried to reason out their reaction in what must surely be air currents, nearly as there are currents in the sea. In the depths of the jungle he watched those birds that run before they "take off", watched their wonderful flight among the trees and cable vines, and countless obstacles in creeper and vine, watched them stay their flight then so surely "land" upon. the branch of some jungle giant. And always he puzzled as to how they did it.

He took his discharge from the *Chevert* at Somerset, that home of pioneers away up at the top end of Cape York Peninsula. From this Outpost of Empire there have sailed many explorers, many expeditions by land and sea, many a romantic adventure.

From Somerset he sailed with Stone on his exploration of the Hinterland of Port Moresby and at a heavily stockaded village came within a hairs-breadth of losing his head. But for a miracle the whole expedition might have been wiped out.

Hargrave shot a pig. He thought it was a wild pig until the villagers came roaring down upon him. He backed away from the excited warriors who, stringing bows and flourishing clubs leaped down the jungle path towards him. To a roar of vengeful voices he hastened in amazement to camp where the Expedition hurried out trying to pacify the natives. But they were bent on clubbing Hargrave. He had killed a pig, and a pig to many a New Guinea native is more valued than his wife. At the critical moment a member of the Expedition snatched up his violin and flourished the bows across the strings. He played with might and main and the lively tune broke in amongst the furious shouts. In a second there was silence as with heaving chests the furious savages stared towards the violin player. And thus the jungle listened to the wonder music of a violin.

It saved Hargrave's life. A big present was paid to the village for the killing of the pig, and all ended well.

But the Expedition moved on hastily.

In the wilds of New Guinea the Expedition met one of the most famous explorers the islands have ever known, the indomitable D'Albertis, famous wanderer of the island seas. He took a liking to the cheery young engineer and invited him to accompany him on a future but very hazardous expedition that he had in mind.

Hargrave accepted with alacrity. So, after a return to Sydney, Hargrave sailed with this little expedition, again from Somerset. And the Coral Seas were bright and blue, the palm-clad islands wonderful.

Clarence Wilcox, a lad of seventeen sailed with them. Two West Indian negroes, a Filipino, a Sandwich Islander, a native of Lifu, and Tiensin, the Chinese cook.

The *Neva* was a tiny launch, now loaded so heavily she was almost in danger of swamping. Hargrave was the engineer, in delight at this chance of seeing waterways and mountains and natives upon which no man had gazed before.

At Moatta Bay they took aboard Maino and his son Waruki, and Dawan as pilots. These three were Torres Strait Islanders. Maino is son of the famous Kebisu, the greatest fighting chief of the Strait. Maino is a great character, he "explored" too with Sir William MacGregor.

Maino is a great old warrior to-day, Mamoose of Yam and Warrior islands.

That was one of the great trips of Hargrave's life, ascending the jungle-clad river for hundreds of miles into the gloomy heart of New Guinea. Here he saw wonderful birds, the quaint hornbill, the beautiful and gigantic Fly River pigeons, the gorgeous Birds of Paradise that danced for him as the tiny steamer chugged along between the dense walls of trees. Ever and anon they passed an enormous Dubu house built high above the earth, its gloomy recesses strung with stuffed heads and painted skulls. Now and again the steamed past the villagers of headhunters and ever and anon stared far up to where houses were built in towering trees. Away up there the people were nearly safe from the headhunters but Hargrave wondered how the monkey-people slept when wild storms swayed their houses. Sometimes a flight of arrows came hissing out of them from the jungle, occasionally they found the river ahead blocked by canoes massed with shouting warriors. He stared at these strange men in their cuirasses of plaited cane, beautiful head-dresses waving as they flourished their clubs to bear down upon the *Neva*. But the discharge of a few rockets and the Neva puffing towards them was sufficient to put these warriors to flight. To them, she must have seemed a terrible thing, belching up their quiet river, puffing out sparks and smoke with her engine kicking up a mighty row. She was a monster and when the rockets came with hissing sparks and thunderous explosions amongst them with dynamite exploding in the river the warriors turned tail and paddled for their lives.

It was a game trip. The little *Neva* puffing up hundreds of miles of an unknown river into the land of many thousands of headhunters.

The *Neva* ascended two great rivers almost to the Papuan Alps, those mighty mountains that tower up into the sky. It was only shallow water at last that turned back the little expedition.

After this trip Hargrave sailed the Coral Sea seeking pearling stations for pearling fleets, roaming the wild Strait in numerous adventurous voyages. There seemed to be no limit to his energy, his hunger to learn all he could of everything that came before his notice. And he thought deeply of all he saw and tried hard to imagine the explanation of things he could not see. These six adventurous years were among the happiest in his life.

And they gave him food for thought throughout all his life.

Eventually, he returned to Sydney and settled down. In 1878 he was appointed Extra Assistant Astronomical Observer at the Sydney Observatory. Thus the lad who had studied the movement of worms crawling along the ground now lifted his eyes to the stars. And far up there, while staring into the starry heavens night after night he pondered at the motions of the air current so far up, and wondered what effect they would have on a machine flown by Man.

How many of our wonderful aviators, soon destined to be flying under the stars at night ever gave a thought to Lawrence Hargrave and his busy mind solving the problems which helped their machine fly through the sky.

Soon, he met a sweetheart. They married. As time went on they had six children, five girls, and one boy, Geoffrey. He loved them all and i t was but natural that he should build all his hopes on the baby son. Alas, what tragedy, that the father's great work should help the means which indirectly brought disaster to the beloved son.

For five years Lawrence Hargrave mapped and explored the heavens. His mind ever was up in the sky. He had found his life work now to he felt certain that man would fly in the sky. He gave up work at the Observatory and devoted hie life to work that was to materially help in the evolution or human flight in machines.

A friend solemnly warned him against this folly.

"Forget it," he warned seriously, "otherwise you certainly will end in Callan Park!"

Lawrence Hargrave laughed. He had a nice laugh, his circle of friends never Left him throughout his life, he could make friends and keep them. This despite the fact that many people declared he was a "crank", and imaginative dreamer who would never do a thing. Such an absurdity, to believe that man could make a machine which could fly in the air. Other people shrugged, others simply ridiculed him and his ideas.

For and all that there were was a tiny circle of friends, of people he never met who believed in him, and continued to believe in him deeply.

Hargrave went on thinking, quaintly working.

This man thoughout all his life gave all his thoughts and discoveries to the world. He refused to patent his inventions despite the entreaties of friends. He wished the world to know the extent of his discoveries so that others could carry on his work towards the grand ideal, that Man could fly.

Alas, he never, never imagined that Man would use these machines for war.

Hargrave, very nearly discovered the secret of dynamic flight. He did pioneer the aeroplane. He published his discoveries and other men patented them.

Besides his keenly looked forward to lectures to the Royal Society of New South Wales and the publication of his papers in their *Journal and Proceedings*, he corresponded with the tiny band of aeronautical workers in England, Europe, and America. This scattered world band were the pioneers of our present-day aviation. And the work of the great Australian was far better known in the busy world overseas than in his own Australia.

It it's a strange fact that in a similar way Australia has not always recognized the work of some of her great sons.

Lawrence Hargrave was well content that other men should use his ideas and where possible, improve on them. Thus would the world build the aeroplane quicker, For he believed that the progress of civilization demanded aerial transport.

But he never thought of War!

2

THE WHIRLWIND

LAWRENCE HARGRAVE combined everything he had ever learned about movements from worms to birds, sea waves to air currents to theories of motion in his mind. He applied this this to his working models. First he made a pair of wings flap by clockwork. After many experiments he made a model that would actually fly. For the power to make the wings flap like a bird he used elastic bands, for those were lighter than clockwork and also he proved that they would, in proportion to their weight, transmit more power.

So that when, years ago he had watched a New Guinea savage draw taut his bowstring, he had not watched for nothing.

That first successful model only flew a few feet, its wings flapping energetically then drunkenly as it side-slipped to the ground.

Hargrave laughed with joy, the richest fortune in the world would never have brought him on hundredth part that joy.

How he had really proved what he had believed from late boyhood, what some dreamers had believed throughout the centuries – that Man could really fly. This tiny model of sticks and paper was heavier than air. It had flown. That flight proved that a great machine could fly. All that was required was the machine to lift it and keep it forging through the air.

Immediately, Hargrave set to work to make a model that would fly further.

French aviation pioneers, 1909.

He made hundreds of models. Soon, he perfected a model with a wingspan of seven feet, and it flew for hundreds of feet. Then be built a man-carrying machine and by doing so proved that a specially-made machine must be thought out and built to drlve it, for the strength of a man was not sufficient to flap the wings.

He kept on with his experiments while the germ of an engine was developing in his brain. With each succeeding experiment he found out a little more, and a little more, and a little more of the many secrets of flight in the air.

Within several years he was building little engines, such clever little things. Some were failures, but each failure taught him something. Then he began to experiment with petroleum. Then he started experimenting with a "screw," instead of the flapping wings. Hargrave "screw" was the forerunner of the modern propeller. His screw was also a propeller but experience has taught us to shape ours much more efficiently. Thus he built his first model of a screw propelled monoplane. It also was propelled by rubber bands which when stretched to the utmost then unwound, supplying the motive power for turning the propeller. He found that a propellor model would fly as well as a fl apping wing model.

Then, he built a tiny three-cylinder engine driven by compressed air. Its weight was but 19½ ozs. Its lightness and simplicity and efficiency was truly wonderful. But the Public still shrugged its shoulders. Called, him a fool. He smiled understandingly, and carried on.

Then made his great discovery. The thought flashed upon him. "Now, if a three-cylinder propeller engine could be made by turning the boss of the propellor into an engine, thus allowing the cylinders to revolver on the crankshaft, the shaft and crankpin being stationary, the thrust would fall direct on the valve face. And this would produce an immeasurably more powerful engine."

He worked at tense speed to make the new engine. It weighed only 3/4lb. He immediately set to work to make an improved one.

Thus he invented the Rotary Aeroplane Engine.

With the feverishly quiet delight of a man who sees all his dreams coming true, Hargrave toiled on.

This little engine, invented by the quiet Sydney man, was the model of construction soon to be used by the early successful aeroplane engines. Perhaps the most famous example was the celebrated French flier, the "Gnome." Other soon-to-be-famous machines were the "Clerget" and "Le Rhone"

How many of us Australians know that the principle of construction of those famous machines came from the brain of Lawrence Hargrave. Even we in Sydney, where his models and engines were thought out and built, hardly know.

 Hargrave now used the propeller as well as the flapping wings in his new models, the engine instead of the elastic bands. Then he wrecked many an ingenious flying model before he found the centre of gravity of a machine. He had to learn this by many a hard experiment so as to ensure the greatest stability in a machine. Again and again he made a model, then flew it only to see the model suddenly dive and crash. A month's hard work gone in a second. He would pick it up, examine it with a rueful smile, find out what had been at fault, then set to work to build another model.

He made a beautiful little single-cylinder engine, driven by compressed air. This little model flew with a cigar shaped tube attached to it appearing so much like a torpedo. Contained in this tube was the compressed air which drove this engine.

The years went by. Hargrave progressed from model to model, improved engine to improved engine. He made a little three cylinder propellor machine and ingeniously counted the number of revolutions made by the propellor when in flight. He attached a reel of cotton on an axis parallel to the screw shaft. Then fixed an empty reel in the crankshaft. Then flew the model. As it flew, so the cotton wound up on to the empty reel. When the model planed to earth he simply counted the turns of cotton now wound to the previously empty reel. By such very simple but efficient aids he learned many a secret of the air, of power and lift end flight. He could count the seconds his models could fly, their distance in the time, their height, and the revolutions made by the propeller. Every experiment taught him a tiny bit more, urged him, go ahead. Sometimes, a failure taught him more than a successful flight. He was very patient, very understanding, very happy. His now growing family adored him.

He made tiny steam engines also to fly his models. He just kept on and on. Then he believed. that the engine difficulty was practically solved. He set his brains to work in an attempt to solve the crucial principles underlying the movements of air and wind and to adapt these movements to help the rise of a heavy machine from the ground. If he could do this he knew that flying machines were   as good as in the air.

He built kites, the famous box kites. Found that they possessed great lifting power. And found that a flying machine with curved surfaces would fly much better than one built with a flat body plane. This intrigued him immensely. He had long thought it, from watching the bodies of birds, of almost everything. The bodies of birds were not flat.

He bad built his flying models with a single, flat surface. Now he experimented with curved surfaces. The results were astonishing. They rose much easier, flew easier. He worked hard to find out the secret, why?, then to apply the principle to lifting a heavier than air machine from the ground.

In one of these experiments, he "looped the loop." Hargrave, so far as we know, was the first man in the world to loop the loop. And he did not do it in a machine. But he, discovered the principle. Had that principle not existed no aviator in the world would ever have looped the loop, simply because Nature would not have allowed it to be done.

Hargrave "looped the loop" by flying a little model built with a curved surface design. To his astonishment the model looped the loop. This result proved at once that a curved surface possessed great lifting power. Hargrave now feverishly carried on with his experiments for this last had taken him a great step ahead.

He made kites that would soar, kites that would lift big weights, a kite that could lift the weight of a man from the ground. He had often wondered at the secret of 'birds so easily soaring in wind and even storm. He tried to find out this secret through his kites. If he could find it then he would. apply the principle to his model aeroplanes. He knew now that he was drawing very, very close to the secret.

Thus the years, went by. All his experiments, all his discoveries, Hargrave broadcast to the world.

And now events began to move fast. In other parts of the world, other men, other nations, were busy experimenting. Germany was experimenting with gliders, England and America were experimenting and beginning to take notice. Surely it would not be a fact that these cranks of the air were right, that Man might really be able to fly! Jealously the big nations began to work, to organise, to watch one another.

Hargrave's experiments were eagerly availed of and he realized. that the great outer world can move faster than we, when their nations and brains and money move with one object. Hargraves was a practical dreamer, a prophet without honour in his own country.

Meanwhile the great forces of the outside world concentrated on the object of flying, accepted everything from the Australian prophet, added his researches to their own, and moved fast.

Hargrave was content to sit back and watch, from a great distance, others carry on. Impossible for him now, with national help while so far away from the centre of operations that were moving so fast and with ever-changing development, to keep pace. He had built the firm, the lasting foundation. Let others complete the work.

He was a glad man when the first aeroplane flew publicly. Santos Dumont flew it in France. And it was simply an arrangement of the Hargrave box-kite. The American authority, Octave Chamte, wrote in his book: "If there is one man more than another who deserves to succeed in flying through the air, that man is Lawrence Hargrave, of Sydney."

Farman and Delagrange built the bi-plane known for years as the "box-kite." Then the Wright Brothers startled the world. They have generously acknowledged their debt to Hargrave.

Hargrave gave to the Sydney Technological Museum some of his original monoplane models, which had actually flown. And a box-kite. These are treasures of our Technological Museum.

But all his other models went to the big Munich Museum, in Germany.

A proposal was made to him on behalf of Germany that a special building would be built for the models, if they were presented to that country. That they would, in Germany, be readily accessible to flying research workers now numerous throughout Europe. That otherwise, if the models were kept in Australia they would probably be of any use to anybody.

This argument won Hargrave. He was a patriot and intensely proud of his work for Australia, the value of which alas, we did not recognise at the time. And Lawrence Hargrave really thought that the flying machine would help bring peace to all mankind.

"In my mind," he said in an address in Sydney, "'that the flying machine will tend to bring peace and goodwill to all; that it will throw light on the few unexplored corners of the earth; and that it will herald the downfall of all restrictions to the free intercourse of nations."

And so, his models went to Munich, Germany.

Alas, it is believed that the dreaded Taube was designed from one of these models.

But the world, nor Hargrave, did not dream of this yet. He was happy in his workshop with his boy son, Geoffrey. Young Geoffrey was taking an eager interest in this rapidly coming science of aviation. Father and son worked proudly, happily. The father was sure that the son would fly, would carry on his own great work, would become an eagle of the sky that he himself had so often dreamed of.

Suddenly, far, far away there came ominous murmurings, then more steadily the grumbling of nations. The guns began to boom.

War!

Geoffrey Hargrave enlisted.

"The Landing, " "Anzac!"

The bullet that killed Geoffrey Hargrave killed the father.

3

THE BUSH LAD BUILDS
THE FIRST AUSTRALIAN PLANE

JOHN Duigan was a quiet bush lad, a thinker and a worker. Any job he undertook he thought out first. Then, with all details finalized in his mind he set to and did the job. Once he had started nothing could turn him aside. No wonder that his father's station Spring Plains, near Mia Mia in Victoria never lacked anything in the up-to-date line that young John could think of and make. No wonder that the station workshop was spick and span, very well cared for tool in its right place, ready for the job. Everything about that station was "modern" and kept in first-class repair, always ready for the job.

Young Duigan decided to build an aeroplane.

The cheek of it.

Why, there was not an aeroplane in Australia. True, a Wright machine was to be brought out for exhibition, it was also rumoured that Houdini and his machine was actually bringing a plane out to fly it. People would believe in Houdini and his machine if it really did fly. But not before.

And now young Duigan - Who'd take any notice of a scatter-brained young bush lad who dreamed he was going to build a flying machine in a bush shed? No-one of course.

We must admit that young John had really set himself a task.

John Duigan, Australian aviator 1916.

The great nations, with all the vast resources at their command were striving all they knew to make a machine that would really fly.

They wouldn't have been flying at all had it not been for a mocked at and unknown Australian, Lawrence Hargrave. After long years he had solved the problem of human flight. Santos Dumont had adopted the Hargrave box-kite system and successfully flown. Voison and Farman used the principle too, Farman actually flew eleven miles. The world went wild with excitement. Then the Wright brothers flew 56 miles.

Man had conquered the air. But this was far away Europe. And now a bush lad was determined to build a flying machine.

Nonsense!

Duigan went quietly ahead, just like Hargrave had done. Didn't give a tinker's cuss for the sneers and laughter of anybody.

All that John knew about aviation was what he had read in a very elementary book on the theory of flight. All he knew about aeroplane construction was from a few details he'd read of about a Farman-type bi-plane. His only guide was a photograph of the American machine of the Wright brothers. But he had his imagination, his clever hands, his resource and ingenuity and – unlimited determination.

For a start, he built a glider. He might learn a lot from a glider and also would really feel what it was like to be in the air.

He knew nothing about gliders except from an odd newpaper paragraph describing some flight of Lilienthal.

But he built a glider, surely one of the first in Australia. He tried it out on his father's station.

Successfully. He glided through the air, above the old bush he loved so well. He was thrilled.

He designed his flying machine. He would build it all in the station workshop.

Except the engine.

'This must be made in a city workshop if he could find a man to make it.

He went to Melbourne. Heard of Mr J.E. Tilley. Tilley was one of the first men in Australia to make petrol engines.

He met Tilley. Tilley became intensely interested in the proposed flying machine engine. They discussed it in detail. Tilley promised to make it. John hurried back to the bush.

He got to work. To make a machine with a wingspan of 24 feet 6 inches, and a length of 35 feet. We would not build a plane today with a greater length than wingspan. But then - we have learned.

And now John Duigan really got down to the job. Not only did he design but he had to design and make every part himself. And think out, then find suitable materials to do it with.

In all Australia there were no aircraft parts to be bought, and no one could build them. Very few people indeed, only an occasional traveller had just returned from overseas had ever seen an aeroplane, so far as that went.

But John's plane hummed on, flying in his mind. He was determined to make it fly in the air. His thought and patience, ingenuity and resource one by one overcame difficulty after difficulty. And the more obstacles he overcame the more absorbed he became in the slowly forming machine. For the woodwork he used ash and red pine, all sticks beautifully seasoned, each one well and truly tested. For the stays he used piano wire, each strand of proved strength. From the steel bands used on wool bales he fashioned the metal fittings. He took infinite pains with the tiniest things, as with the largest part. On a solitary run the success of his machine might depend, perhaps life itself. Everything that he put into that machine was not only first thought out as to efficiency but was tested thoroughly for suitability and strength as well.

Slowly but surely the machine began to take shape. It was a

labour of love. He was with it throughout all the daylight hours, working in the shed until far into the night. And then it remained in his dreams as he slept. He was determined that machine would "go."

It was a marvel of ingenuity that this lad was building, putting together part by part so that the whole machine would be a model of lightness, efficiency and strength. There was not one solitary nail in it, nor a tack, nor a screw. Every piece was firmly bolted together. No glue was used. This machine had to rise in the air, to be a practical dream of stability and strength the builder was resolved that vibration would fail to shake it apart.

With care and precision he fashioned the wheels and propellor shaft. People now came to gaze at it, to wonder. It really was beginning to look like something. Surely it would never fly!

John Duigan even made the ball races, his mind and cunning hand-fashioned everything, right there in the station workshop with the crows carking up in the old red gum outside.

Only the shock absorbers and the propeller had to be made in the city.

It was the first aeroplane propeller ever made in Australia.

When it arrived, it was a great day at the station. Carefully, John tried it on the propeller shaft.

It would not fit!

He had to re-shape it, re-balance it, and recover it himself.

The engine arrived. In delight, he carefully unpacked it, carefully place it on the workshop bench. For a long time he examined it. And frowned.

It was a good engine, yes. An ingenious engine, yes. He had no fault to find with the making.

But was it entirely suitable for lifting a machine above the earth, then propelling it through the air?

He doubted it. He had learned so much, thought so much when he was experimenting with the glider, and in making part of the machine. He realised now how very different our efficient aeroplane engine must be to other engines. It had such a very different job to do.

Over this truly ingenious machine John thought long. It was a kind of motor cycle hybrid. In it were the magneto of a single cylinder engine, and a distributor from a 4-cylinder engine. It was air-cooled. John frowned.

This extraordinarily adaptable station lad started to improve that engine. Utilising improvements that developed in his mind and putting them into the engine by aid of the tools in the station workshop.

Then studied the engine again. And frowned yet again.

The engine was not sufficiently powerful, its air-cooling system. also was inefficient. John worked it all out in his mind, figured out the capabilities of this engine in his mind then, in imagination, fitted it into the machine and took it for an imaginary flight.

And saw that his loved machine would only just tip-toe along the ground.

John fitted larger cylinders to it, changed the air cooling system to one with water-cooled heads. Then hand-bored out the crankcase, and cast and made a water-circulating pump. Tried the engine, was dissatisfied. He changed the drive from a belt to a pulley and smiled approvingly when it improved the job. He tried her out again and proved it could be further improved. He designed and made a radiator, a big job it was but quietly and methodically he went on hand-soldering each of the 500 cooling fins.

This was all designing work in the first place, while in the carrying of it out it was highly skilled work.

The bush lad did the whole job single-handed in the station

workshop. Even today, thirty-years later none but the most completely equipped engineering shops in the Commonwealth would or could undertake so big a task.

Came the great day when the plane was wheeled out for its first trial. All the station rolled up. John swung the propeller, turned it several times.

It spun, stopped, spun again, spun faster. There came a splutter and roar from the engine as the propeller whirled fast.

The station dogs belted for the wide spaces.

John climbed aboard. Toyed with a few mysterious gadgets, let her go.

There came a roar and a bust and a mighty jerk that was the envy of all the buckjumpers in the paddocks. All that had happened was the propellor shaft had wound itself up.

With a whimsical smile John climbed from the machine.

"Something has bust!" he remarked.

His station friends looked dubious.

John examined the machine.

"I'll have to make another, and a much stronger propeller shaft," he mused.

He stood back, gazing, calmly working out in his mind all that had taken place, and why.

"This is an 8 foot propeller," he mused.

Even today, thirty-years later none but the most completely equipped engineering shops in the Commonwealth would or could undertake so big a task.

Came the great day when the plane was wheeled out for its first trial. All the station rolled up. John swung the propeller, turned it several times. The machine has a 24 foot wingspan. It really is a toss-up whether the propeller revolves and the machine stands still, or the machine goes round and the propeller stays put."

Duigan in his Wright brothers type G bi-plane.
Duigan's own pusher bi-plane.

He laughed. Then wheeled the machine back into the workshop and started thinking out how to rebuild the propeller shaft and improve the whole plane.

On 16th July 1910 he made the first successful flight, the first flight ever made by a machine built in Australia.

It hopped a whole 24 feet!

What a thrill. The biggest old man 'roo on the station was hard pressed to out-distance that.

John Duigan was well pleased. If this machine of his brain and hands would hop 24 feet in a stride then with improvements it would fly.

Methodically he set to work on improvements.

Two months later her tried her out again.

She flew one hundred yards.

He improved again.

At the next trial she rose to a dizzy height of twelve feet and flew 196 yards at a speed of 40 miles per hour.

He improved her again, and she did fly. From the Bendigo racecourse, flights of three quarters of a mile.

John Duigan's bi-plane is now a proud exhibit in the Melbourne Technical Museum.

Those days seem far away, 1910-11. We can be proud of the Australian lad who then, in a bush shed so far, far away from the old world whose vast resources were only just enabling it to fly in timid little hops of five and six miles, designed, built and piloted a flying machine that would really fly.

Three years passed. Overseas, the nations were feverishly advancing with their flying machines. Machine after better machine came rolling out from the workshops of America, France, Germany England.

The Flying machine had really come to bring an historical change of development in the World's progress. Then came war.

John Duigan enlisted in the Australian Flying Corps.

There were only two other pilots senior to him in the date of their licence (Oswald Watt, licence 112, you read of him here as our beloved Legionaire and W.E. Hart, no. 199, No. 1 of Australian Licence.)

John Duigan very soon became Captain John Duigan M.C., of No. 3 Squadron, And fought many an air duel before he was badly wounded.

During April 1918 No. 3 Squadron got into continuous and very heavy fighting, assailed by Albatross and Pfaz scouts immediately they took the air. From the growing intensity of artillery fire on the ground the Heads guessed that something big was doing. The war birds had to find out quickly what that "big" was.

The weather was very bad, mists hiding the activities of the busy armies away down on the earth, while scudding clouds afforded ideal hiding places for lurking enemy hawks of the air. Desperate duels daily were fought in hide and seek battles amongst the clouds while down below on the flats of the flats south of the Somme fresh enemy batteries were continually coming into action, pounding the British, French and Australian lines. Up above, flying blind through the mists our war birds fought the Albatross scouts then diving low sought to pierce the mists and locate and bomb the enemy batteries. That a great attack was threatening was soon to be proved by the great assault by the Prussian Guards. One gusty morning Captain John Duigan with Lieutenant Patterson as his observer were flying low over the enemy lines staring down in the search for camouflaged batteries. Through a lift in the mist Duigan thought he saw something suspicious and diving low down almost landed on the mighty German railway gun getting ready to fire from Harbonnieres.

John Duigan at the controls of his biplane 1911.
The Red Baron's coffin (painted by 3AFC in PC10 Aircraft Green) was lowered into his chalk grave at Bertangles Cemetery on 22 April.   Duigan is assisting with holding the foot of the coffin.

It was a great find, and great good fortune that they lived to tell the tale. They got clear away and went tearing back to the 'drome with the news and action was quickly taken against that huge menace.

The diggers soon captured it, in the last great push of the war.

You can see that great gun now – in Canberra.

In the next few days after they'd located the big gun, No. 3 Squadron was constantly engaged in reconnaissance duty, bombings, and dog fights with a vicious energy who was all out the British machines from the air. Every scrap of information that the war birds brought in had only been obtained at the risk of their own lives. Some fine Australian lads lost the number of the mess in these hurricane engagements but not without first doing fearful damage to the enemy machines.

John Duigan was soon to be blown out of the war. He with Patterson were speeding through the mists seeking for shafts of sunlight through which to photograph the German lines. Several times they caught a glimpse of a ghostly machine but it was gone as soon as seen, back into the mists. Then brighter sunlight came and they got to work flying low while taking no notice of the Archies bursting around them. Photo after photo they took of busy enemy activity below, the placing of new guns, the movement of supply columns, the arrival of reinforcements, the digging of advanced trenches. Through the roar of the motor, the bursting of shells, the two Aussie war birds worked on, perfectly satisfied that they were doing good work. Their R.E.8 flew over Villers-Bretonneux and Patterson's camera was very busy registering the hive of martial activity down there. Suddenly Patterson's camera closed with a snap as four enemy tri-planes dived upon them. A tri-plane hurtled past with guns flashing as Duigan roared her up to the challenge while Patterson bent over the machine gun. A quick burst from the enemy and the fight was on.

They zoomed and dived and manoeuvred in a terrific speed of whirling machines while bullets flew like hail whipping through the fabric. Duigan handled the plane magnificently striving to return to his own lines with the photographs knowing how tremendously important they were. The information contained within those photos might mean the continued existence of a Division of Australian infantry. As determinedly as he had battled to built that tiny machine but a few short years ago so now he handled his war machine to bring to safety those photos upon which rested the lives of men.

Patterson, crouched over his gun was firing steadily, determinedly, cooly.

The four enemy machines were all over them, it seemed a collision might come at any moment.

A tri-plane suddenly side-slipped, fell away, her crew riddled through with bullets. In an avenging roar the three remaining machines closed upon the R.E.8. In a furious hail of fire Patterson suddenly slumped forward, recovered.

Gritting his teeth he worked his gun again, badly hurt. Bullets struck Duigan and he dived away from the fight with clenched fists striving for consciousness, grimly determined to reach the British lines or die at the controls.

He skimmed in over the French lines and landed on a flat near Cachy village. He refused to have his wounds attended to until his precious camera plates were hurried to the Squadron aerodrome.

That was the spirit that has made our young eagles invincible in war and peace.

Captain Harry Cobby in 1919.

4

THE FIGHTING ACE

LIEUTENANT Harry Cobby of No.4 Squadron, Australian Flying Corp, loved England. Everyone here was so good to him, it was a dear old country too, he was very, very glad he had come 12,000 miles to fight for it. With a smile of delight he "double-sheeted" the blankets of half a dozen of his messmates, then tiptoed away. He had got even. with those jolly old galoots, anyway.

Cobby's bright blue eyes could fairly dance with fun. But the time was fast coming when those eyes would narrow to the glint of the tiger for this laughing young Australian was destined to become an Australian Fighting Ace.

And the Fighting Aces, be he British or New Zealander, Canadian or French, South African or Australian, American or German, were terrible in the air, famous on land.

The lads toiled through months of ground training in England, but very little flying. Planes and pilots were too desperately needed in France.

Cobby had not yet fired a shot in the air, had not three hours actual flying experience when he found himself in France.

France! the lads thrilled to the new land. Everything was so new in this one of the oldest of lands, everything so different to far away Australia. Soon, they heard the boom of guns. Glanced at one another, laughed. Soon then they gazed up at the first Fokker, droning overhead.

They too, would soon be up there, with shrapnel bursting all around them.

Vicious machines, those Fokkers, piloted by grim eagles.

And then – they saw their first "Circus".

Coming with a roar from the skies these fiery red machines hurtled their challenge from the air.

"They're like comets!" whispered one of the lads, "and, oh my! How they can fly!"

Magnificently handled by their proud war aces these deadly machines sought fight, always fight. It was all they were built for, all that their terrible pilots craved, was fight. Cobby gazed up breathlessly as these scarlet, demon painted painted machines of the proud Richthofen roared by.

Terrible machines, terrible men. The Australian fledglings stared as the scarlet menace roared away. Then glanced at one other.

It was a great sigh to have seen the famous Richthofen Flying "Circus."

The time would come when they must face these ruthless demons of the sky.

Cobby wished the time would come soon.

But their Flight Commander was an experienced man. He worked them like slaves, hard training for the grim work ahead.

"You can't fly! You can't shoot!" he snapped. "You're only in the baby class. You're not playing at soldiers now. Here's where you learn to work."

He had no intention that his fledglings should be torn to pieces by Richthofen's eagles. When his boys did take the air they would be able to look after themselves. He'd jolly well see to it.

Which meant "Hard Work" for No. 4 Squadron.

Up to this time there was no British or French "Circus" but one was now just ready to take the air. Famous Aces like McCuddin, Ball,

Bishop, Monk and the French Ace Cuynemer were forming the daredevil squadrons that were to soar up and smash Richthofen and Albatross circuses. That time was here now, when the very air would roar with the great battles in the skies.

The enemy had first developed the Circus idea, fast machines manned by star airmen cruising the skies on no other duty but to pounce on our machines and blow them to pieces. No wonder that the Australian Flight Commander insisted that his lads should get in every practice possible before they soared to meet the proud superflyers of the circuses.

The No. 4 Squadron worked hard indeed. Theirs was a single-seater fighter Squadron, equipped with Sopwith Camels. Tricky little machines to fly, obstinate too as a camel if you didn't know how to fly them. Very difficult to shoot from, surprisingly difficult to hit anything while flying the bucky things.

Much more so when an angry Fokker was blazing away at your tail. But the Camels when mastered proved splendid machines. No. 4 Squadron with these machines was destined to make a big name for itself.

"Now that you can handle the machines – more or less," snapped the flight Commander, "you've got to learn to shoot. If you don't the only wings you'll be flying with are your own." So that marksmanship, and then formation – flying was drilled into them.

The Commander was very particular in "formatting", following the leader, flying in formation, obeying orders in the air. For a flight going into action is something like obeying orders in the air. Very like a Fleet at sea. Every machine must keep its own place and line, be ready at the instant to carry out any manoeuvres signalled by the Flight Commander. Just as battleships and cruisers and destroyers must be ready to obey an Admiral's signal. If the flying men are not in position and instantly ready to obey orders swift defeat may be the result.

Rene Fonk, the Allies's greatest flying ace, shot down 45 aeroplanes.

Major Arthur Holroyd O'Hara Wood, died in action over Saint-Quentin in France on October 6 1918.

In learning this, tragedy came to C Flight. The five machines in the air, practising formation flights. The young pilots quietly gazing down on the line, when the Flight Commander put them into a steep dive. Something went wrong. As the machines flattened out two of them collided with a crash, interlocked, and hurtled down to another machine. All three pilots were killed. It was a black day for the Squadron.

A terrible tragedy that brought home to the lads the imperative necessity of being ever alert, of quickly learning to handle their machines, of being ever prepared for any movement dictated by the leader, or forced on them by or to outwit an enemy. And it also trained them in skill and initiative towards the time when they would be flying alone.

They learned lesson after lesson. Very soon experienced British pilots were saying "You No. 4 chaps certainly can formate."

And then – they ventured out over the enemy lines. Cobby, pilot in the rear machine in a patrol of five.

His job is to keep his eye on the leading machine, to protect the tail of the machine in front and watch out that no enemy dived on his own tail.

Suddenly – a noise like a falling comet – sharp, metallic, clattering of machine guns and a patrol of

Albatross scouts had mixed it with the two rear machines. As Cobby swerved aside while training his gun he noticed the machine ahead swerve violently, it had got it in the engine, immediately it began to fall out of formation with the pilot desperately striving to right it.

"Shall I keep formation?" wondered Cobby, "or shall I turn and fight?"

He followed behind the falling machine with his own guns blazing, protecting That machine as it fluttered nearer and nearer the ground. The other machines had sped up, their pilots unaware of the hawks that cut off the two rear machines. Thus the young pilots learned an unexpected lesson – that machines dawdling too far behind can be "cut off" and probably destroyed.

Cobby protected that gliding machine all he knew, terribly worried as to whether to leave his distressed comrade and follow the formation, or turn and attack the pursuers diving at his tail. He was dodging wonderfully, putting up a great fight. But perhaps it was fortunate for him that the attackers were inexperienced fliers too.

The problem was quickly solved. The stricken plane came to ground with a great bump. Cobby saw the pilot leap out – unharmed. He was taken prisoner.

Cobby, almost on German soil now zoomed straight up into the sky seeking his vanished "formation." Could not find them. With the pursuers still at his tail he fought his way back to the lines. Except that his comrade was taken prisoner he had enjoyed the little scrap. It gave him great confidence too. With a little more experience he would know instinctively Just what to do on the instant, no matter how tight the corner.

A flying ace must be born that way otherwise he never becomes an ace.

A few days later and O'Hara Wood avenged the captured Australian by shooting down a German D.7.W. two-seater. They watched it tumbling down to crash near La Bassee.

The first victim to No. 4 Squadron.

There was a celebration in the mess that night.

No. 4 Squadron was now definitely "in the air." Their serious interest in war had started. With the keenest rivalry too far now No.2 and No. 4 Squadron shared the same aerodrome and the pilots vied against each other for the Squadron honour of bringing down the most enemy machines. It was a terrible game in which these lads were engaged, the game of War. No-one would have thought it, to meet the happy-go-lucky crowd on the ground.

One cloudy afternoon Cobby in company with two other machines was soaring over the German lines in quest of prey. He felt it just the very afternoon for a fight, eagerly he appeared ahead, to right and left and above.

His fingers were fairly itching to press the trigger. He couldn't wait, he slewed away towards Lys and there reared up before him a great big sausage balloon, an enormous fellow rolling gently in the sky. In sheer delight Cobby dived with his gun blazing and the balloon collapsed with a mighty grunt and swiftly wobbling down in flame. and smoke. Laughing fiendishly Cobby looped the loop to show his disdain of the anti-aircraft fire and then, with his blue eyes dancing sped up, up, in search of sterner prey.

Peering out from the plane his eyes suddenly narrowed to a steely glint, he crouched over the controls and the plane roared around.

Out from the clouds some distance away droned four Fokkers. Three of them were flying at 10,000 feet. There was a fourth flying about 1,500 feet below them. They were heading towards Merville. They vanished among the clouds, hadn't seen him.

Cobby acted instantly and with the cool daring that soon was to make him an Ace. He made straight towards those Fokkers but flew under the clouds so as to approach them unseen. He was smiling eagerly, fairly trembling with excitement. Here was a chance to prove himself – one against four.

Great hiding places the clouds, they gave an aeroplane wonderful cover for a game of hide and seek. Rapidly Cobby overhauled the unsuspecting machines that presently emerged from a cloud only to fly on into a cloud He trailed them as a hawk does its prey that it is watching down there upon the ground. He wanted to pounce on the lower machine. Soon, his chance came. He was speeding on hidden in a cloud just able to see the ghostly machines lipping through the vapour ahead. In a moment he would emerge from this cloud at the precise moment that the three upper Fokkers would begin to fly above a big, fleecy cloud. That cloud would then be between them and the lower Fokker.

At the precise moment Cobby hurtled straight down. And this is what was to make him so terrible in many a battle. Diving a terrific speed he crouched over the controls and gun but held his fire until it seemed that in a fraction of a second he must crash into the Fokker. He fired a sudden burst at only 50 feet range and the Fokker collapsed straight down into a bed of clouds. Cobby hurtled down after it but it had gone for all time, crashing far away down there.

Something flashed past his tail as guns chattered viciously and the three Fokkers were upon him hot to avenge their comrade. He sped for the British lines twisting and turning like a bird harried by hawks. They failed either to catch or hit him. No wonder for he was a better airman than they.

There was joy at the 'drome when he landed. He had added another tally to the bag of No. 4 Squadron.

Perhaps fortunately for the youngest of the Australian Squadron the weather was extremely bad for flying and fighting. Mostly the Squadrons was in reconnaissance duty, finding out what the enemy was doing behind his lines, photographing his positions, and in bombing raids. By the time the weather cleared the young pilots could handle their machines almost with the best. Then came vigorous movement between the opposing armies and No. 4 Squadron was fighting constantly.

Cobby very speedily proved himself a daring but level-headed pilot. He won promotion.

One morning Cobby was in charge of ten machines in two formations, he with his five scouts leading while Courtney with five others flew just above and behind him. Courtney's flight was to watch the tails of the leading flight lest hawks dive upon them from the higher sky. A dense mist over the earth, it was only with great difficulty that the pilots could keep formation. They could not have done so had they not

Cobby in his Sopwith Camel while instructing in England, c.1918–19.
The high-visibility check paint pattern is Cobby's own handiwork.

Captain Cobby with his Avro 504k.

been now trained men. The invisible machines flew on weirdly quiet for the fog seemed to blanket the drone of the motors. Cobby stared anxiously ahead lest at any moment they run into lurking patrols. Whatever happened they must see the enemy first. Occasionally through a drift in the mists away down below they would see the vague outline of an enemy balloon. It would vanish as they were swallowed up by the mists. After half an hour's flight Cobby began to wonder where he really was. There was no means of telling. A very little more of this and he might be leading a lost patrol. It was eerie there in the mists, just the deadened droning of the machines steadily slipping through the mists.

He led the flight lower to 4000 feet hoping to catch glimpses of the earth. The mist was not so dense down here. Presently, a balloon loomed up. In a slight clearing of the mists he spotted another, and soon afterwards another. He determined to follow this line of balloons until he saw some familiar landmark and then strike away towards home.

And just then three Albatross scouts appeared gliding through the fog just below them. Scarlet machines!

They vanished into the fog. Following them now appeared a line of Pflaz scouts – scarlet! Then more Albatrosses.

Richthofen's Circus!

Cobby gave the signal for action by rocking his machine fore and aft then dived straight down into the centre of the enemy formation. The flight roared down after him.

In an instant a hurricane fog fight was waging madly in the mists. Cobby sent his first machine crashing then pounced on another as Pflaum poured bullets into a stalling Albatross. Robertson and a scarlet plane disappeared through the mists half-rolling back upon one another. Elwyn swerved then poured bullets into a scarlet scout as it overshot his machine then as it half-rolled back at him a Pflaz roared down upon him from behind with guns blazing. The three whirling machines swept down through the mists but Robertson downed his victim and came zooming after another. Cobby was on the tail of another scout that almost collided with a third machine only to fall away the next instant a victim of Cobby's bullets. Scattered throughout the mist planes were whirling in mad fight to the vicious chatter of machine guns, roar of motors at full throttle, flash of hurtling machines.

By now the leaders of the scarlet machines were far ahead, serenely sailing through the mist unaware of the fight behind.

The survivors of the scarlet machines slipped away and the mists followed them. But far below six of their machines were blazing upon the ground.

It was a great win for Cobby's flight but he was glad indeed when he got them safely back to the 'drome. That fight in the mists had been maddeningly exciting but getting home was a ticklish job.

Just didn't No. 4 Squadron celebrate *that* night.

Captain Cobby (centre) with officers of A Flight, No. 4 Squadron AFC, and their Sopwith Camels on the Western Front, June 1918.

Austral extras to a British Bristol, 1917.

5

THE GREAT RAID

AND now came days and weeks of stirring excitement not only for No. 2 Squadron but for all the British and Australian Squadrons. For the Germans made their mighty attack on Bapaume. Ceaselessly all day long was the tremendous thunder of the guns. At night, far as the eye could see the gun flashes were vivid lightning illuminating the many miles of country. Under this terrific pressure one of our hard-pressed armies began to give way. Ceaselessly the flying birds attacked the advancing Germans crowding into Bapaume from every road. If ever it was to be now was the time the flying daredevils must help protect infantry and artillery, give them every chance they possibly could. A Squadron of course was in the thick of it, bombing Bapaume and its packed roads. And the Fokkers roared down upon the war birds while the masses of German infantry below scattered for their lives. They had good cause to, hearing that hurtling roar coming down through the mists above with ever and again a blazing machine crashing down amongst them. There came the screaming of racked propellors as the battling machines dived and wheeled, twisted and turned with Robertson bringing down a Fokker in a pall of smoke that leapt into flame as the wreck crashed down upon a scattering battalion of infantry. Horse transport bolted in mad terror, motor transport collided and capsized. Up there beside Robertson was Cobby pouring lead into a zooming, diving, Albatross that suddenly stalled then went into a vertical nose dive and crashed amongst other bolting transports while men fled from the spinning wheels and maddened hoofs. Then another roar as No. 2 Squadron hurtled into it and a Fokker and a Plaz came crashing in flames. Day after day the Squadrons bombed and fought over that packed Bapaume-Cambrai road shooting up the advancing enemy and machine-gunning his travelling artillery and dense masses of transport. He hit back ferociously with his own war birds and downed numbers of our own machines - the Squadrons after a hard day's fighting would return to the Mess to silently toast those who nevermore would answer the roll-call. But now our own "Circuses" were breaking the enemy in the sky and losses daily were growing more serious than ours.

Cobby and his daredevil mates liked tensely throughout those hectic days and speeding through the air while staring down at this awe-inspiring sight of one great army hurling itself against another. Masses of men and machines interlocked in a struggle to the death across a ruined countryside. Wherever the machines flew there was visible through the mists the dull glow of scores and scores of villages in flames. Sometimes high up in the mists they would fly into dark, warm clouds that was but the smoke haze from the burning towns below.

Earth and sky was filled with rolling thunder, flashes of thousands of guns. And above it all, diving down into the very heart of the melee the war birds came roaring night and day.

One morning after the great Push was over, Cobby and his cobbers were in the air seeking what they could destroy. Slowly but certainly the air filled with huge, fleecy clouds, the hunters could see nothing but their own misty machines. Presently they came down through to find that below them was a light mist and through this they could see they could distinguish the ground, and presently a railway line. Cobby flew lower still and saw a train come puffing along. With a "Whoop-lah" he dived and his machine-gun rattled bullets into the engine then back along the length of the train. She got up speed in hasty puffs but Cobby had wheeled and was rattling back along over the train again with his gun beating a busy "rat-a-tat-tat-tat." He chased her right into the station where his cobbers swooped, dropping bombs which blew up two ammunition trains and a goods shed piled with war material. Heavy military lorries rumbled away from the station and the boys livened these along with a hail of machine-gun bullets. Laughing while dodging the Archie and machine-gun fire they zoomed up into the clouds again, seeking other victims.

His cobbers loved to follow Cobby for with him there was always "something doing."

Next evening coming home after a slow day Cobby saw a two-seater plane spying out our artillery posts. He dived, giving it a sharp burst as he flashed by behind, instantly rising up in a stalling attack underneath its tail with another sharp burst.

And down went the plane.

As easy as that.

But he knew how.

So expert did the war birds become after a very few months flying and fighting. They had to. Otherwise they did not last.

Next morning was a dawn hunt, the Flight split up. McCloughrig and Jones-Evans flying in company almost ran into a Rumpler two-seater. They attacked and the startled machine rattled by, bullets coming in furious bursts, crumpled and fell away down into the mists. Almost immediately two Pflaz scouts dived upon them and the four planes wheeled and stalled, zoomed and half-rolled and dived in a desperate double duel. Suddenly a Pflaz crumpled up, fell away. His mate sideslipped and vanished. A little later and McCoughry spotted another cruising hawk. He dived and took it with his first burst and it slipped inside then nose dived at terrific speed. Air fighting is very sudden. One moment you're in it. The next, unless you're very slippery, you're not.

Next morning Trescowthick and Cobby were flying in company. As with half open throttles they droned towards the German artillery lines they laughed and waved at one another pointing towards a long line of observation balloons now commencing to bob as the crews below hastily began to haul down on the cables. If there was any mischief Cobby loved it was to strafe these big balloons. And didn't the enemy know it! As the two machines came droning along Archies burst near them with reports like rapid thunderclaps bursting in palls of black smoke. The two Aussie daredevils opened to full throttle and dodged in lightning zig-zags to deceive the aim of the gunners then Trescowthick chased the enemy plane guarding the balloons while Cobby dived at the fattest balloon he could see. The great big fat thing was jerking and bobbing in frantic alarm as the crew below hauled down the cable. Cobby grinned fiendishly and fired a burst into it then wheeled to loop the loop as the balloon collapsed in flame. He laughed at the sight of the little men away below running like hares to dodge the falling cable. Just to hurry them along he swooped with a roar and lathered them with machine-gun bullets then zoomed straight up and darted at another balloon. Having enjoyed their little bit of fun the daredevils flew away chased by Archies now bursting at such close range that the machines slipped and wobbled in the terrific air blasts.

Soon they spied three Pflaz scouts disappearing into a cloud ahead. With a whoop and wave to one another they crouched over the controls and dashed into the cloud on the tails of the unsuspecting machines.

A fighting pilot's life may be a short one. But exciting.

They came out of that fight with their tails still in the air, but full of bullet holes.

Next afternoon Watson and Cobby in Camels were flying in company at 6000 feet over La Basses. Watson was a happy-go-lucky,

Pilots of No. 1 Squadron, Palestine, 1918.
The officers of No. 2 Squadron in 1918, Cobby third from left, front row.

laughing young Australian and like Cobby, a first class fighting pilot. Eager for prey they stared among the clouds as their machines droned on. And then they spied five Pflaz scouts cruising among the clouds some distance away. The scouts were also looking for prey but had not spotted *them*. The two Australians immediately climbed up into the clouds eager to trail the enemy, and pounce. But they tracked him very cannily for they must take the five by surprise otherwise they'd butt into a hornets' nest. The fighting enemy pilots were good ones and not even an Ace could afford to make a mistake. When the two Aussies judged they should just be just above the invisible enemy they dived straight down through the clouds.

And there were the five Pflaz machines serenely sailing immediately below them.

Then from the clouds only a short distance away there emerged a formation of enemy tri-planes.

Watson and Cobby continued their dive, each had singled out a victim. Cobby held his fire until he was glaring right into the startled, upturned face of the enemy pilot. Then his gun fired a furious burst and the Pflaz trembled violently, fell away, then spun whining down to earth. Watson's attack also took his enemy by surprise and down the Pflaz went in a terrifying spin. Cobby was now duelling with another Pflaz and while the two machines were tumbling and rolling over one another Watson was fighting for his life against the other two. There came a thunderous roar as the enemy tri-planes dived to attack and just then Cobby, with his guns blazing saw the two wings of his enemy collapse as with a violent explosion the machine broke up in the air.

It was time to be off.

Cobby and Watson fell away like stones from among the avenging tri-planes. At terrific speed they dived down through the clouds almost to the earth and then, flattening out, sped for their lives.

They dodged the enemy and came laughing back to their drome.

Thus every day brought its adventure and hairs-breadth escapes to the boys of No. 4 Squadron, as it did to all Squadrons. And each day each Squadron board proudly chalked up its tally. No plane was counted unless it had been seen to crash. Many a machine brought down out of control must have failed to return to the enemy lines but if it was not actually seen to crash, it was not counted. The rule was very strict.

Cobby loved the fun of leading his flight high above the clouds then seeking out and diving straight on enemy formations. He had long since perfected many a trick in air fighting, tricks to deceive an enemy pilot while in flight, tricks to deceive the gunners of the anti-aircraft batteries, tricks to beat the balloon barrages, and tricks to beat rifle and machine-gun fire from the ground. Machine-gun fire from the ground is especially dangerous to a low flying plane. And the boys often had to dive low while shooting up enemy roads and trenches. A fighting pilot to live, must quickly learn many a trick, think out tricks of his own, must be ever alert to constantly outwit enemy tricks. For the daredevils of the air on both sides were not only cool and brave men but were very cunning ones. They did not only take their machines into the air and look for a fight but they thought deeply while off duty when back at the drome. Thought out ways and means to beat an enemy under all circumstances, thought deeply on their last flight and seldom failed to learn something from it. Thu, on every succeeding flight a good pilot had become just a little better than he was before.

Perhaps one of Cobby's proudest moments was when he led his own Flight as the spearhead in the first great raid against Haubourdin. An honour indeed for a young Australian pilot. A great responsibility though. But what a thrill to live through. The wing-commander was Lieutenant-Colonel L.A. Strange. The big fleet was made up of many

British and various Australian Squadrons loaded heavily with bombs and ammunition, pilots and observers keyed up to concert pitch. Squadron after squadron took off and roared ever higher on the big climb, glistening formations of man-made eagles perfectly handled. Each Flight in layers of machines three thousand feet above the other. As the force sped on towards La Bassee Cobby thrilled to the mighty drone throbbing through the air. When over La Bassee the formations dipped prettily to lose height, Cobby stared down, he was in the lower formation and at the head of his own Flight must now lead the attack. Three thousand feet above him Murray Jones leading No. 2 Australian Squadron now flew in left hand circuits awaiting his turn to follow Cobby. Above No. 2 Squadron circled the British Squadrons.

Cobby dived, and his Flight roared down after him. They smashed a Fokker as it frantically rose to escape and carried straight on to the great hangars rising up to meet them. When almost on the roofs of the hangars they flattened out, released their bombs and spouts of flame shot up from the earth as explosion after explosion shook earth and sky. Hangars, machines, barracks, workshops going up in a holocaust of flame and smoke. Squadron after squadron now came roaring down in a riot of destruction. Through the inferno planes sped, raining machine guns into stationary planes, into workshops and transport, and all the beehive of a great aerodrome and supply depot. They set it as a hive of activity, left it wrecked and an inferno.

Cobby and his daredevils in their lighter moments enjoyed diving from a height and chasing troop trains, swooping down and plastering the crews of the anti-aircraft batteries, and diving too at the big clumsy balloons. And acting as decoys, a risky game.

He and other skilled pilots were chosen to fly low over the German lines, flying slowly and uncertainly as if they were "green" pilots taking a look around. Very soon a formation of enemy machines would chase them, each machine eager to bring down the fledglings. Then the decoys in apparent confusion would turn and hastily try to escape.

But in spite of their apparent clumsiness they were flying cleverly, swiftly but unobtrusively gaining both speed and height. They pursuers at their tail flew all the more eagerly the closer they gained to their quarry that was so tantalizingly near, keeping Just out of effective range. They left their throttles out to the full not noticing they were being drawn up into the clouds.

And then - a roar and hurtling of machines as the the ambush dived upon them while the decoy machines suddenly turned and with guns blazing helped them spinning down in ruin.

6

SKYLARKING

OCCASIONALLY they had "great fun". Went pirating on a "special mission" as they called it.

"How about a pleasure cruise?" grinned Cobby one morning.

"What's doing?" enquired Malley.

"We'll leave our 'cards' on the Lille aerodrome," answered Cobby, "and maybe pay a little visit to Lille. It's a lovely morning."

"I'm with you," said Crosse eagerly, " you can't leave me out of this."

So they strolled to the drome to load up with their 'cards', leaden ones.

Lille was the big old French town now in German hands. It was a hotbed of dromes, mechanical units, Headquarters and guns.

Like a bolt from the blue the three planes swooped down upon Lille drome. Two Albatross scouts were on the tarmac, ready for flight. The war birds dived on them with guns blazing and in seconds both enemy machines were on fire.

Aviators, mechanics, groundsmen were pointing, shouting, running. Crowds came out of huts and tents. The three planes dashed around the drome firing at everyone they could see. Pilots, mechanics, cyclists, everything with legs was diving into the hangars and sheds with the roaring planes at their heels. The boys were having a great time, swooping past the open doors of the hangars to blaze into the great sheds, rattling their bullets into the doors of huts and chasing men under cars and kitchens and wherever they could scurry. When not a man remained to be seen they flew laughing across the drome tarmacs with their wheels skimming the ground then zoomed up and flew just over the roofs of Lille. From the streets the people stared up amazed at the sight of these runaway Australian planes. The pilots yelled and waved and many of the captive French citizens waved back, shouting hysterically. Past chimneys and over tree-tops to skim over gardens and streets the wild planes flew with a brazen roar. By now sirens were blaring, machine-guns chattering from roof-tops, excited German soldiers were firing from the streets, the forts began to open up. Dogs were barking, fowls scattering, birds set up a twittering to join in the excitement, But the planes kept just over the roofs, twisting and turning and easily defying the gunners until they skimmed over the town outskirts.

Then they flew low to the ground. And thus the guns could not be brought to bear upon them.

As they flew on they still drew more laughs as from military barracks German infantry came pouring out to wave at the planes that had skimmed their hut roofs but they ducked and dodged and ran like startled rabbits when the machine-guns barked.

Groups of training infantry got the shock of their lives as the roaring planes almost knocked their caps off with their wheels. There was a wild scatter from parade ground, after ground, with amazed officers staring up then run or get their own heads blown off by the wheels. The planes flew onto swoop over troops leisurely engaged on various duties. Those troops stared petrified as the planes zoomed up with the pilots looking down their tails with their fingers at their noses to the officers. Then down they'd dive again and terrified squads of infantry would fling themselves flat to the ground gazing up to seethe pilots blowing kisses at them.

It had been a great lark. The three pilots flew back to the drome well pleased with themselves.

The crack German Aces all had their machines brightly painted with fantastic figures representing demons charging through the air, or open-mouthed sharks, or other grotesque figures that lent their machines an absolutely terrifying aspect. The British pilots generally carried some decoration also, though mostly in the form of a mascot. Cobby, while on leave in England had "souvenired" two notices from a train. One read - "Caution - it is dangerous to lean out the window." The other was "Please do not spit." He had screwed these notices one on each side of the fuselage. It was grim humour. Cobby roaring into battle against a scarlet monster with his own plane plastered with homely English notices. Above these notices were his favourite mascot, painted figures of Charlie Chaplin.

The boys were great on souvenirs, they tried hard to souvenir a huge Great Dane one pitch dark night but the dog, very willing to come, could not get over the high fence. At the critical moment the whole family came pouring out with torches and guns. And the souvenir hunters vanished.

They tried then to souvenir a group of statuary in the centre of a French town. It was a nice, dark night, the town was quiet. But the statuary was very heavy, very cold to handle, and tightly cemented to the town square. In the middle of the digging operations the gendarme came running along and the the conspirators vanished quickly.

The envy of the four Australian Squadrons was the really great souvenir owned by No. 2 Squadron.

An aeroplane!

It was a French two-seater and where on earth they souvenired it from no one would ever tell. Proudly they called their mascot "Sophie." They kept Sophie well-hidden lest visiting French aviators spot her. They Frenchmen would have been amazed even though they knew the Australian by this time. There must have been a terrible row and a great mystery on some French drome when they found an aeroplane gone. No one could put an aeroplane in his pocket, and they knew the Germans had not taken it. But that plane was gone. They never found out where she vanished to, nor who took her.

The strain of war is terrible. To these young war birds in their constant fighting at terrific speeds often against appalling odds whether above the clouds or skimming the ground, the nervous reactions were terrific. Only the strongest constitutions could stand up to it and even these must break up in time. Little wonder then that these high-spirited boys let themselves go whenever there occurred a chance of fun.

Otherwise many a war bird as time went on, with his nerves shot to shreds, must have gone mad.

No wonder Cobby and his cobbers, when on mischief bent, made the most of it. On leave one time in Edinburgh they played up, Cobby with two others borrowed three hansom cabs, climbed into the drivers' seats and went at a spanking trot down the main streets. The citizens turned to stare then laughed as with whips cracking, drivers tally-ho-ing the cabs came racing by. Those drivers wore the uniform of the Air Force and their chests were bright with ribbons. Edinburgh had never seen such cabbies.

But who do you think these cabbies picked up as fares? No less important personages than the members of the Japanese Trade Mission, then visiting the Scottish capital on important business. But these Big Men from Japan thoroughly enjoyed the joke.

A few days later though, one of the jokers gave the citizens a huge laugh. Cobby and he and all of them were staring up at the great memorial statue in the centre of the city, admiring its tall beauty.

"I'll climb to the very top of it," declared an ambitious pilot.

"Bet you you can't!" declared Cobby.

"Right. If I lose, I shout the best dinner in Edinburgh for the crowd. If I crown the monument, then you foot the bill."

"Right," grinned Cobby.

And the lad began to climb. A very ticklish job, shinning up those glistening columns of marble. A crowd quickly began to gather until, as the lad climbed higher and slowly higher the great square became filled with thousands of people, staring up.

He got right to the very top. Perched there dizzily, he waved his cap to the crowd. They laughed and cheered, thinking it great fun.

And then - the climber couldn't climb down.

He tried his hardest, he just couldn't. And they couldn't do anything to help him.

The Police had to call out the City Fire Brigade. These came with a clatter and clang and ran up the big extension ladder to the rescue.

And didn't the crowd cheer!

And didn't the war birds laugh!

Captain Cobby, D.S.O., D.F.C., and two bars, was to finish his war record as Acting Major Cobby, credited with an official tally of 21 enemy planes and a number of balloons. And hero of a score of desperate enterprises.

7

ROSS SMITH

ROSS Smith was a hefty South Australian lad, well-liked by his cobbers. A great worker, he was also ready for a mischievious prank if anything "was doing." Mixing work with fun was a joy to the lad.

He enlisted during the first week of the war. Soon, he was fighting on the grim slopes of Gallipoli, learning that Johnny Turk was a first-class fighting man. From the battle-scarred heights of Rhododendron Spur he was carried on a stretcher. Next, he found himself in Egypt. When he came out of hospital he climbed the Pyramids to signalize the event. From that dizzy height he made faces at the Sphinx far down below. But that dignified old Sphinx kept its face smiling out over the desert and took no notice. The Sphinx was a favourite with Ross, he used to wonder what was the secret of its smile.

"Laughing at the little men," he smiled one day to a friend, "I wonder how many armies, how many nations the Sphinx has smiled at as they passed this way."

Presently, he found himself in the Sinai desert again fighting Johnny Turk. Ross battled with the Light Horse in the moonlight bayonet charges at Romani, the stubborn fighting in the oasis at El Katia, and then the terrible campaign that pushed the gasping Turks far back across the merciless desert.

And then Ross found himself an observer in No. 1 Squadron of the Australian Flying Corps.

Captain Ross Smith, flying Ace.

Captain Ross Smith (left) with his observer and a Bristol F2B fighter
in Palestine February 1918.

This lively lad quickly made numerous friends. His always cheery smile, his willingness to work or laugh, his ever-helping hand to a comrade carried him far. Besides, he was soon to prove that he was a splendid pilot, absolutely fearless, always ready for any venture.

None then knew that he was going to be one of the world's greatest pilots, and that Australia was to be very proud of him. We will describe but a very few of his exploits but then tell you about the Big Flight.

Lieutenants Ross Smith and Roberts, escorted by Murray Jones and Ellis in Martinsydes did the first big reconnaissance far to the rear of the Turkish armies in Palestine. A great feat that fired the whole Squadron to go exploring over this battle-torn land whose every mile breathed the romance of ancient history. A brilliant day as they soared away above the rugged hills, the grim valleys, the precipitous wadys running like huge red scars across the land. The green of olive trees and barley fields, the encampments of Bedouins, the pretty villages of Jew and Christian, and the old-time sacred towns. Beit Jibrin, Bethlehem, Jericho, Jerusalem - names that stir us all.

Had not some Great Man when a boy in far off times away down there declared: "And they shall fly in their chariots!"

The war birds droned on, intensely interested as they gazed down, taking military photographs while ever alert for fight. Again and again Archies came at them to burst with a thunderclap amongst a fleecy little cloud of smoke. They saw below them the enemy armies with active troop movements, clouds of dust arising from the hoofs of cavalry, a busy railway stretching across the land, a German aerodrome away behind Beersheba. And yes, there was another one, poked away down there among the hills. It was a great patrol, a cheeky patrol. The enemy never dreamed the flying birds would dare to come cruising so far away behind their own nests.

And when they rose up to intercept them they found they could not do it.

That highly successful flight started in earnest the big bombing patrols and ai battles which at last drove the German aviators beaten from the Palestine skies. But great battles were to ravage this land before all that could happen.

Later, there came a day when Ross Smith and Kirk flying together beside Paul and Weir in Bristol Fighters had just "shot up" the Nablus railway station. That cheeky little stunt had brought no end of excitement and damage to the infuriated Turk. He had lost quite a number of men not to mention a bolting train or two and a fine railway station that was now a heap of rubble. When the German fliers came speeding for vengeance the two cheeky Aussie machines had simply turned their guns on them and shooed them away. And now they were looking for more trouble.

They soared over the Jenin drome as if they owned the place. There could easily be a score or more German planes down there - what did they care! They circled the place at their leisure marking out the lay of the military camps, noting the nice big fat dumps of ammunition simply inviting a bomb raid. They took photos so that they'd know exactly where to drop the bombs during some nice, moonlight night.

Then a nest of ambitious Turkish machine gunners opened fire with a Hut-tut-tut-tut and the two Aussie machines dived and came roaring down to the challenge. They scattered the machine gunners and came roaring to the aerodrome quite ready to fight if a trap was set for them. It was, but it didn't quite come off. A staff car suddenly appeared going full speed past hangar after hangar with a Staff captain shouting orders. Five scout planes were suddenly wheeled out with engines roaring but the Aussies dived straight at them and plastered them with machine-gun bullets. Men fell and scattered around the planes as the Staff car came hurrying back only to be met with bullets and chased away into a shed. It hit shed with a terrific bang.

Those five machines never rose from the ground. When the Aussie machines had finished with them they couldn't.

The Aussies circled the drome for twenty minutes waiting for other machines to venture out, meanwhile putting in time by firing at every man who poked his nose from cover. Bullets were whistling around them but the Archies couldn't get a clear shot for the machines were speeding so low in around the hangars. When sure there was nothing further doing the Aussies flew insolently away, followed by Archie shells.

Not long afterwards they staged another private war on Nablus and then "shot up" the Balata aerodrome. They got away with it then soared up seeking seeking what further they could annoy. Ross Smith saw a string of horse-lines on a flat sheltered by a hillside, with a line of small camps not far beyond them. With a laughing signal to his flying mate he swooped and chased the Turks from their camps. As they ran for the hills the two planes chased them and enlivened their pace with bullets. They laughed to the spurts of dust around the heels of the fleeing men, those Turks had never run so fast in their lives. The war birds next swooped on a barracks from which was coming an angry crackle of rifle fire. Kirk plastered these riflemen well and truly then turned their attentions to a line of marching troops. These grey-clad heroes scattered for the hills as if on very urgent business while the swooping planes, the pilots laughing with a cheery wave to one another sauntered home just above the Lubban road. There was no telling who they'd meet.

They met horse teams and motor transport loaded with munitions. They opened out the throttle and swooped down. Bolting horses and stampeding motor lorries soon littered the countryside, that roadway looked as if a cyclone had suddenly burst upon it. As a finale, the boys "shot up" a big crowd of Turks just returning to bivouac and enjoyed the pleasure of chasing these too into the hills.

All in the day's work.

Next morning at dawn Ross Smith and Kirk were again early birds, in a Bristol Fighter flying 11,000 feet over the Wady et Auja that looked like a big black chasm away there in the earth. The sun came up in glory. Suddenly they spied two early hawks, Albatross ones. The Bristol Fighter got straight into them.

There was a ding-dong scrap with quick rattling of machine-guns in the sky. Then an Albatross dived like a stone. Ross Smith was on his tail in a flash sure he was only shamming "dead." So he was. Bullets ripped through the Australian fuselage from the Albatross diving behind them when only fifty feet above the ground the first Albatross had to instantly flatten out, or crash. He flattened out. But Smith pressed the triggers and then - the Albatross crashed - definitely.

Smith did a half-roll back on the second Albatross but it fled. A great chase. The Albatross skimming the ground doing all the pilot knew to shake off the relentless pursuer. It skimmed the broken banks of a precipitous waddy then darted along the Nablus road to swerve and make for a rocky hillside. Up and over hilltops then down the other side just skimming the rocks but wherever it went its terrible pursuer was close behind. With both machines at full throttle the roar brought the Turks tumbling from their dugouts to see what was doing. With short bursts coming behind him the desperate pilot again and again kicked his rudder bar from side to side to shake off the terror behind. To no avail. They flashed past rocky corners and left tree branches violently swaying in their airstream but still the chase raced on. At last Ross Smith got his Albatross. It crashed right down upon a Turkish camp.

The time was fast coming when the great battle of Nablus was to shake the plains of Armageddon. But this story will not describe that nor other furious battles that racked the blood-stained fields of Palestine.

We tell but a few lighter episodes in the life of Ross Smith. Several of his most interesting flights were when he flew Lawrence of Arabia to and from his Headquarters in the desert, to the Headquarters of General Allenby.

Lawrence, one of the most romantic figures in desert history now had gathered his army of Arabs fairly close to the British right flank, with the object of joining in the coming battle at the right moment. Ross Smith, together with several other Australian aviators were sometimes detailed to fly out in the desert, locate the Arab army in hiding from the Turks and bring its fearless leader back over the enemy lines for consultation with General Allenby. Lawrence of the steely eyes soon took a liking the capable young aviator.

And Ross Smith was able to repay his interest.

For the German air hawks at Deraa discovered the Arab hiding place in the rocky hills. And what they did to that hideout with bomb and machine-gun fire was just too bad. Two B.E.12 machines were stationed with the desert raiders but the Germans quickly put these two out of action and Lawrence's Arabian cavalry took to the hills.

Lawrence sent in word quickly, asking for some modern Australian machines to come out and save the situation. Peters and Traill, Ross Smith and "Pard" Mustard, Headlam and Lilly were ordered to flight out into the desert and protect the Arabs. When the Bristol Fighters arrived, the Arabs came down from the hills and greeted them enthusiastically. But when Ross Smith arrived at Um es Surab in a giant Handley-Page the tribesmen went wild with delight. Swarmed around it in hundreds, then thousands, firing into the air, dancing and yelling delight, roaring defiance at the far away German aviators.

And truly, the German eagles got a shock when they arrived for an easy victory next morning. The Aussies were sitting down at breakfast when an Arab yelled that the enemy were coming.

"Of course, they *would* come just now," said Smith disgustedly, "and me enjoying breakfast too."

They stared up at the rapidly approaching drone.

"Two Pfalz scouts, one D.7.W two-seater," frowned Mustard, "what a miserable crowd to interrupt a man's breakfast. We'll dish them up and return before the coffee gets cold."

"I'm going with Ross," declared Headlam, "I'm fuller of fight than I am of breakfast."

And they strolled across to their planes watched in breathless excitement by thousands of Arab eyes.

The opposing planes dived at one another and the machine-guns rattled. The D.F.W. got it in the engine, faltered, stalled, dipped down with a pilot desperate at the controls. His observer was dead. The pilot just managed to land her, and the machine went up in flames. The other machines fled.

The war birds returned to their breakfast frantically cheered by the Arabs, A big sheikh had himself seen to it that the flying heroes breakfast was kept warm.

They were enjoying an after-breakfast smoke when the Arab look-out yelled in delight.

Three more Pflaz were coming.

"Well," drawled "Pard", "I suppose we'd better get aboard and give these Arabs their treat. I notice they've all got box seats."

Every rock on the hillsides was tipped by an Arab, all tuned up for the fight to start.

Ross Smith and Mustard roared up to the challenge. In an instant the battle had joined in whirling machines in furious fight. Suddenly, to the Arabs yell of intense derision, the enemy machines turned and fled, the Australians on their tail. Two landed near a little desert railway and hurriedly taxied along the ground to the shelter of the

Turkish Outposts. The Australian machine soared up and chased the third. It travelled all it knew back to its drome at Deraa where Archies and ground defences opened up on the pursuer. The Australian machine wheeled around and flew back, and defying the fire from the Outposts, dived down and machine-gunned the two machines still sheltering on the ground. They could see the faces of the machine gunners as they hurtled by.

That afternoon there was another yell from the Arabs as a German D.F.W. suddenly swooped down. To a wild scatter the bombs came whistling then "Crash!" "Crash!" "Crash!" "Crash!"

Peters and Traill ran to their machines and with motors full out soared up. The D.F.W. fired a few bursts then wheeled and at full throttle raced back for its drome at Deraa. The Australians caught it just before it reached home. There was a sharp fight with the D.F.W. desperately flying to reach shelter. Suddenly it faltered, then went down in smoke.

Australian machines then bombed the Deraa drome and wrecked it.

Thereafter, Lawrence's Arabian army was not troubled by German hawks from that quarter.

Within eighteen months Ross Smith had been made a Captain. For conspicuous gallantry on numerous occasions he won no fewer than five decorations, the Military Cross, then a bar to it, a Distinguished Flying Cross, and two bars.

And his cobbers declared he earned them all.

8

EAGLES OF PALESTINE

FRANK Macnamara was a Victorian lad. He never dreamed he was going to win the Victoria Cross. But he did dream of flying. He wanted to get his hands on the controls, to fly and make his name as pilot and navigator in these newly made flying machines of Man.

Already, he held a commission in the Militia. War came, he enlisted in the Australian Flying Corps. He sailed with No. 1 Squadron, for training in England. Soon, he was in Egypt, a fully-fledged war bird. Then he found himself flying over Sinai while the Light Horse and New Zealanders, veterans of Gallipoli were fighting the Turks on the desert below.

Romani – El Katia – Bir-al-Abd – Rafa – Maghdaba. Desert battles far away fought on sands whence once the Roman legionnaires bled and died. Stubbornly the Turkish armies fell back with Australian war hawks watching them from the sky. Bitter fighting across more than a hundred miles of desert and then – the green fields of Palestine.

The British and Australian warbirds during those hectic campaigns were a lively crowd of daredevils and had every need to be. Otherwise the German fliers would have wiped them out then played havoc with the mounted troops. For the German machines, those vicious Taubes and well-armed. Fokkers, the Aviatiks that hurtled down like hawks were then much superior machines in speed, climbing, manoeuvering and fighting power than our old B. E. 2.c machines.

The Turkish camp at El Arish, 1916.

The town of El Arish, 1916.

But their men weren't superior.

Our old machines held good man, only boys in years who with the greatest cheek tackled the superior enemy machines wherever they could find them, chased them from the skies. It was not until 1917 that the German aviators came with a furious attack to regain air supremacy. But by then it was too late, our lads had now the Bristol Fighters and S.E.5's. There were many desperate struggles in the air before the enemy were definitely beaten, never to regain the air supremacy they might have held all along.

Pluck and daring had eventually beaten the machine.

And now in 1917 the Germans and Turks, in new machines were desperately striving to blast the British and Australian warbirds from the air. They hadn't a hope for our lads full of confidence and now in new machines daily took the air with a cheery wish for adventure. They got it – in plenty. Times were lively, events moving fast. The mounted men had crossed over into Palestine and were rolling on to the great attack on Gaza and Beersheba. Both sides were working their war birds all out in an attempt to down the other fellow and thus hide the great movements behind their own lines. The Turks and Germans were rushing up reinforcements, suddenly too their Air Arm was increased and viciously attacked the British 'dromes and machines. The Australian war birds now lived days and nights of excitement. Some of the lads were shot down and killed, occasionally an unfortunate one landed only to crawl out of the   smash and be taken prisoner. There was nothing the Australian airmen or mounted man hated much as to be taken prisoner by the Turk. In all the countries upon which that Great War was   fought   very, very few Australians

Captain Frank Macnamara, V.C.

were taken prisoner. The Turk made but a very, very occasional capture.

When the Turkish infantry retired from Wadi Sheikh Nuran, Lieutenant Turnbridge was doing a nice Patrol over Tel el Sheria, just sailing low seeing what he could see down in the seething Turkish antbed below, thinking of anything but being made a prisoner of war in Turkey. He very nearly was, just escaped by the skin of his teeth.

Jacko's anti-aircraft guns barked viciously and a violent explosion under the Aussie machine threw it in the air like a feather. Tunbridge spun away in the stricken machine desperately fighting for control and height. He coaxed his wounded engine all he knew to carry him far back over the Turkish lines. He fled towards Fafa like a bird with a broken wing. He just managed to keep her in the air and sail away back out over the lines, and away past their mounted patrols. And then the machine came down in the wastes of No Man's Land. He crawled out from the machine, revolver in hand, and gazed quickly around.

Not a sign of life. Far away, the boom of gunfire towards Beersheba, dying in a low thunder towards Gaza. Around him were low hills, brown and barren under a blazing sun. Miles away came relief to the eye in the green of barley fields.

But not a sign of a Turk, not an Arab.

In great relief Tunbridge took his bearings, cautiously set out to walk to the Australian lines. He knew they must be a good many miles away.

He was intensely alert, fearing to meet an Arab patrol. He thought grimly of those hawk-eyed roamers of the desert, and of the tracks he must make. He knew that if hostile Arabs caught him they would cut his throat.

He had no water and it was very, very hot.

A jackal sat up and snarled at him. It seemed as if the beastly, cowardly thing knew he dare not fire his revolver, for fear that wandering Arabs might hear.

Next day, a metallic eagle of the sky was soaring low away out from Rafa, also looking for enemy patrols. Lieutenants P.S. Snell and Morgan stared down for what they could see. And Morgen panted, then whipped up the glasses as they glided lower.

Something down there, a man, staggering along, falling, rising, staggering again but keeping on, on, on. They circled over him, he looked up, waved eagerly.

"It's old Tunbridge," shouted Morgan "all out too!"

They landed, picked him up, and flew away home.

Again and again the same thing happened. But sometimes the distressed war bird was caught by Turk, or Arab. If Turk, it was all right, he was generally treated well. But if by Arab! well – it was a fifty-fifty chance.

Only a day or so later that a Fokker roared straight down on the El Arish aerodrome. McNamara and the lads held their breath, it was a complete utter surprise.

But instead of a bomb she dropped a mailbag. Then zoomed straight up to the skies and away.

In the bag were letters from two Aussie war birds captured several days before and a letter too to a German aviator captured by the British.

A reply was sent, the Aussie machine sailing down to within fifty feet of the German 'drome. They waved to her from the ground, she waved back.

Such little courtesies relieved the grim business of war.

Frank McNamara was singing, singing away up in the moonlight. A night of utter beauty over the age-old fields of Palestine. Just the drone of the raiders, the stars and the light and the moon.

Raiders! the rush of a camel host with the coming of the dawn.

Such has been old Palestine throughout the centuries. But now!

The modern raiders droned on and Lieutenant Frank H. McNamara was singing.

He often used to sing when in the air, to sun or stars or moon. His fellow officers had long since got used to the singing pilot, "old Mac" would follow on, he'd be sure to fall out of formations but he'd be there when the whips were cracking. He always was.

He did fall out of formation. With his eyes to the stars he was unintentionally climbing – climbing. Suddenly, the plane stalled. Mac grabbed at the controls, instantly came back to earth. He would have done so pronto had he not wakened up.

He brought her out of the downward spin then raced after his cobbers who now were flying far ahead like tiny points of moon kissed steel. He only just caught them up as like an avalanche of doom they dived roaring straight down upon the grim redoubts of Sheria.

"Crash" "Crash!" "Crash!" "Crash!" Splashes of flame, spouts of earth rushing up to meet them.

Roar of Archies, ribbons of flame from machine guns then thousands of flashes of rifle fire. Above the roar of motors, the thunder of bombs, the crash of exploding Archies the air seemed alive with countless bees. And the whirling, diving, zooming bodies of planes. Bullets ripped through wings and fuselage as the raiders dived and turned, zoomed and swooped while:

"Crash" "Crash!" "Crash!" "Crash!"

Then they were away into the outside night and there was Mac still safely at the tail of the formation singing up at the moon.

Several days later and they were at it again bombing Junction Station, a vital Turkish supply point lying down between the brown hills near Beersheba. Just at a critical moment when over the Turkish redoubts Heathcote's engine stalled. Desperately he strove to right it, falling, falling, down to the Turkish lines. The engine spluttered as Archies burst in fleecy clouds around it, they followed him down thinking the plane might just recover in time. But with a sickly wobble the machine came down in the Turkish lines and Heathcote was taken prisoner. Sympathetically, his mates flew away chased by bursting Archies. His mates could do nothing. They waved him good treatment and God speed to Constantinople.

They fought them in between blinding duststorms, pleting the miles of Turkish trenches with bombs and machine gun fire. Like great moving clouds the Anzac horsemen were rolling up out of the plains, the Yeomenry were riding on Sheria, the New Zealanders were coming fast, the British infantry were advancing to attack the terrible Ali Muntor redoubts that shielded Gaza.

Gaza, city of Samson. Over these plains had marched the armies of the Philistines, the hosts of Persia, the legions of Rome. And now had come the Anzacs. Above this ground over which had galloped the chariots of the Assyrians the Aussie warbirds now sped through the air.

From the glow of a dying duststorm they again roared down on Junction Station, flashing birds of steel soaring down through exploding bursts of shrapnel.

And a British bird was shot down. He crawled from the wreck and hurriedly put a match to his machine. As black smoke welled up, Turks came running from trench and redoubt. But there was a roar through the air and a machine swooped down, landed. The pilot ran for his life with bullets tipping the dust at his feet.

"Steady!" called Baillieu to the racing pilot, "you've got time man but watch your step!"

Ross Smith laughed.

Smith was Ballieu's observer. He leaned from the machine and reached out an arm to the exhausted man and pulled him into the plane as it roared off.

Machine gun and rifle bullets drilled the machine's tail and wings. But they were in the air and away over the very rifle muzzles of the Turks.

A very game rescue. How strange that the next day almost on the same spot the episode was to be repeated so dramatically. "Under desperately circumstances," so declares the official report.

Above the hills of Beersheba fleecy clouds were bursting so prettily. Among them the war birds were circling and diving to crash their bombs yet again on Junction Station. From the Turkish redoubts came a long sustained, furious burst of fire.

Frank McNamara was enjoying himself tremendously even though a fragment of shell just fizzed by within an inch of his head. An Archie opened out before him and the Martinsyde swerved violently. McNamara laughed while gazing down at the blazing station, at the smoking redoubts, the trenches lined with men whose white faces against their rifles were staring up at the sky.

Then "crash!" and the world seemed to explode for McNamara in a blaze of flame. With the clang of a busy factory ringing in his ears he was falling, his fingers frozen to the controls. Then light flashed again and consciousness fully returned. He dragged the machine out of the spin and gasped for breath. The Martinsyde was under control – good. He became aware of a nasty pain in his leg, felt warm blood drizzling down to his shoes. Carefully, he moved the leg. Thank heaven! It was not broken.

Then Rutherford's B.E.2.c. was hit, McNamara saw it stall like a frightened horse then slip away from a cloud of smoke. He caught a glimpse of' Rutherford frantically working at the controls, falling away down there in between the hills right between those two big redoubts.

McNamara clenched his teeth, with a roar the Martinsyde sped down following the wounded machine. And the earth leaped up as they fell into a roar of fire. When almost on the ground Rutherford's engine suddenly picked up, her nose turned upward, McNamara. held his breath. But too late; the machine was too near the ground, desperately it strove to rise, faltered, landed.

McNamara roared down beside it.

Rutherford leaped out, ran to McNamara, climbed aboard.

McNamara worked the controls, suddenly desperate. His wounded leg was numb. Desperately he willed movement into leg, the Martinsyde roared, began to rise.

McNamara pushed at the rudder bars, his eyes blinded with pain. The Martinsyde taxied – crashed.

Rutherford leaped out.

"Hurt?" he cried.

"No," gasped McNamara. "Give us a hand old man, this dashed leg won't act."

Rutherford helped him out in a hurry, he put his foot to the ground.

"The leg simply has to act," he grinned. "Quick! Fire this machine while I limp across to yours."

Macnamara convalescing after the event.
Macnamara's flying gear.

Turks were leisurely climbing from the trenches to either side of them expecting an easy capture. Suddenly, flame, then smoke poured from the Martinsyde. Then Rutherford was running to the B.E. 2, McNamara was painfully climbing aboard.

A cry of alarm from Turkish officers, the prey was escaping. Shouts as soldiers came running, stutter of a machine gun, sudden whistle of bullets. Then other machine-guns burst in, joined by a quick rattle of rifle fire.

With his heart in his mouth Rutherford swung the propeller. To his almost hysterical joy it started at the first swing. He leaped for the machine to see McNamara coolly shooting at the Turks with his revolver. The machine lurched, roared forward, taxied straight at the nearest advancing Turks. It took to the air at their very heads and they fell flat to the earth.

In a hail of rifle and machine-gun fire the plane soared drunkenly up between the two lines of redoubts. Struts were cut by bullets, the fuselage was riddled. But she cleared the ground, flew on, wobbling desperately.

But McNamara got her back to the 'drome. He had fainted when they ran to lift him out.

And that is how Frank McNamara won the bronze cross for Valor.

9

A Soldat of the Legion

THE throb of a distant drum, tramp of marching feet, the blaze of a desert sky and a wild defiant song. The column of moving men burned brown as the pitiless sands, the little colonel marching on ahead. What men! Great-hearted men fierce as the merciless Touareg, men who laughed at death, trained to fight to the bitter end, men who fought madly, loved wildly, men who lived but to do and die.

Men of the Foreign Legion.

A sudden shreik, thundering hooves, screams of a Touareg charge. A bugle call, the calm shout of the colonel to his beloved rogues. "Aux armes! Aux armes!" and the Legion form into Battle Line.

Only Death can break those ranks.

In such a memory picture we often think of our own loved Legionnaire, Lieutenant-Colonel Oswald Watt, O.B.E. Legion D'Honneur, Croix De Guerre – and Australian Squadron Leader.

May I tell you about this.

He loved the bush. He grew into a fine strapping lad, six feet of laughing boyhood. And he carried himself with and air.

But he wanted adventure. And he got it. Joined a Scottish regiment and looked the very thing in kilts. Everyone liked him too, they could not help it. Soon he was Captain Oswald Watt, A,D.C. to the Governor of New South Wales..

He became intensely interested in the new science of flying. He and the tiny band of Australian enthusiasts learned all they could. Then he went to England and joined the Bristol Flying School. He learned to fly. In 1911.

Oswald Watt with his Bleriot monoplane in Egypt early 1914.

Oswald Watt - Legionnaire 1914.

This good-looking lad was doubly fortunate in that his Dad was well-to-do, with growing Australian business interests. So the young fellow bought a Bleriot monoplane. What crazy machines they were! but how he loved that comical kite. He took it to Egypt and flew over the Pyramids and zoomed down over the smiling old Sphinx. Many a flight he had alone far away over the desert sands.

He took the machine to France. In that fair land everywhere were serious faces,

Whisperings, the rumbling of a coming war. If it came, the young Australian was going to be in it.

He sought to enlist in Aviation Militaire of the Foreign Legion.

The Legion laughed harshly. Grim-faced they stared at this big Australian boy who as grimly stared back. They decided they might take him – if he were a man!

He sneered back and laughed.

"Try me!"

"Baby," they replied harshly, "do you realise they truly say of us that we are the Legion of the Damned!"

"I'm not damned!" he laughed, " and you cannot damn me. Try it!"

"Right!"

And immediately he realised he was of the Legion.

He was shorn or all class distinction. He who was an Australian Captain and had been Aide de Cong to the Governor of New South Wales, Australia. Now he was but a number, and only a recruit at that. He was Soldat deauxieme Watt. Posted to Bleriot Squadron No. 30.

Soon he loved them. Grudgingly, then freely, they grew to love him. And to show it in their own rough manner. Soon they called him "Capitaine".

Time passed. Under the sternest discipline Soldat de deuxieme Watt became a real soldier of the Legion

And War came.

Beating of drums. The rumble of guns. And a town burning in the night.

Soldat Watt was transferred to No. 44 Squadron, destined to become famous in the French Army.

But oh, at the start of that war what crazy machines the war birds flew! The Legion flew Maurice Farmans, clattering old crates we would call them today, they would look quaint in a museum. But in these pioneer machines the pioneer fliers fought and died.

Those first machines were so low-powered that it was dangerous for the pilot to attack land objectives in them, the engines were so feeble that the planes could rarely rise high enough to be clear or rifle fire from the ground, So clumsy were they to handle and maneouvre that the observer when shoot1ng at enemy machines was delighted at his good luck when he scored a clean hit. And what do you think! they fought with rifles and revolvers in the air.

How different to the roaring monster of 400 miles per hour of today armed with its armour plate and crew and cannon, multiple machine guns, tracer and explosive bullets and shells. And parachutes. There were no parachutes alas for the doomed men in a stricken machine in 1914-15.

But what a grand crowd were the pilots of No. 44 Squadron, fliers of the Legion. Bearded, moustached, clean shaven. Laughing men, quiet me, grim men. Men of various nationalities but all   with one thing in common – a coolly reckless bravery always seeking fight.

And Soldat de deuxime Watt soon shone among them all. He might not best their bravest but their bravest could never beat him.

This little story cannot tell you all his adventures whilst a Soldier of the Legion. We can only glance at a very few episodes then pass on to his other adventures only to hurry these to hurry to other great men.

One morning the young Australian was above the German lines when five German machines dived at him from all angles. In a whirling dogfight he quickly shot one down and put another out of action. With the roar of a machine diving upon him with another roaring up from below, he wheeled to fight, a hawk at his flank when a crashing blow turned everything into blinding flame. His machine slipped, spun down as he fought for feeling in his hands to pull her out of the spin. He regained control when almost sure to crash and his battered machine skimmed drunkenly back over the French lines. When they pulled him from the machine blood was pouring down his head. He waved them back when they wanted to carry him, on the arm of a French poilu he walked to the casualty station. The doctor attended the wound, gave him the bullet as a souvenir, ordered him to hospital.

And the Soldier of the Legion refused to go.

A week later with bandaged head he was in the air again. A Taube dived with a roar, others came at him from all sides, the ambush had been waiting away up in a cloud. Again he shot his way back to the French lines with the soldiers in the trenches blazing up at the pursuing Germans. He landed safely – with the main spar shot through!

A miracle. How the crippled machine had held together in the air puzzled even the experts.

"The Australian soldat leads a charmed life," declared a staff officer.

"Nonsense!" frowned a stiff moustached old colonel, " the soldat is a man of the Legion! And the devil looks after his own."

Watt overheard, and smiled.

He knew that it was the God of Battles who had shielded him that day.

Perhaps his most exciting adventure was one day when he did not even have the thrill of a fight. He was soaring above the enemy lines, on reconnaissance duty with an Observer. Keenly they observed the battle-scarred country below seeking hidden machine gun nests and camouflaged artillery. For from some well-concealed position heavy batteries had roared into action, playing havoc with the French lines. All around the countryside was now the sullen murmuring of the guns, sudden spouts of earth and debris from bursting shells. But the special nest or artillery that the lone scouting plane was looking for was now discreetly silent. The plane was rocking now, around her was bursting with ear-splitting crashes anti-aircraft shells in beautiful, fleecy clouds of smoke. Ever and anon, above the roar of the engine came the screeching whistle of fragments of exploded shell. A splinter smashed through a strut to a vicious vibration, a hole appeared suddenly through the tail of the machine. Calmly the two airmen gazed down at the enemy lines.

Suddenly, a great silence, a terrifying silence.

"Crash!" "Crash!" "Crash!" and screaming fragments of shell.

Deathly silence.

The engine had stopped.

"Crash!" "Crash!" "Crash!'

There was nothing for it.

Desperately Watt fought for height as the machine rapidly glided down. Would they clear the German lines! He doubted it. No Man's Land rapidly rose up to meet them all pockmarked with shell holes, staked with broken strands of barbed wire, a broken, burnt-out cottage, a No Mans Land of desolation littered with the flotsam of war. To Watt's astonishment he saw a big haystack still intact right in the centre of No Mans Land.

And then – they were hurtling over the top of the German trenches, skimming the very parapets. Astonished faces stared whitely up at them, they heard the startled shouts of officers as they crashed, the machine with her nose in a shell hole, her tail in the air.

Watt scrambled out and sprang to help his observer.

"Hurt old man?" he shouted.

"Don't think so! Winded a bit," gasped the struggling observer.

"Quick!" said Watt and snatched at the man, hauling him out.

A machine gun stuttered, rifle shots came and then the Germans were climbing shoulder high in the trenches firing excitedly, machine guns started barking as the crews hurriedly trained them from the trench tops. The French army opposite dare not fire lest they hit the men running towards them.

"Put your best into it," shouted Watt; "head down and go for your life. The marathon of our lives, old man."

Instinctively he was racing towards the haystack. Machine gun bullets now whistled around them, in moments these bullets would come in a hail. Watt glanced around; the observer was staggering white-faced, gasping for breath. Watt turned back. The observer waved him away.

"Save yourself comrade," he gasped, "never mind me! Vive la France!"

"What th' hell!" shouted Watt fiercely, "insult me like that! When we get back to the lines I'll punch your head off! Come now, run, run!"

He flung his strong right arm around the hurt man and almost carried him at the run, leaping around shell holes, struggling over tangled wires, racing on – on. Not for nothing was the Australian soldat known as one of the most powerful men in the Legion.

They reached the haystack, buried themselves in it, the observer layback weakly smiling, gasping great breaths. He had been badly shaken when the machlne crashed.

"The Legion," he gasped with a smile, "Always – does it."

"Yes," frowned Watt, "and you just wait until I get you back to the lines! I'm going to give you the hiding of your life."

"When I get - my wind," smiled the Observer, "I'll fight you – now."

"That's the spirit," laughed Watt, "wouldn't it be fun to stage a fight in No Man's Land. How the Legion would cheer!"

They lay listening to many little soft patterings, little thumps, little squeaks, little sighs. Hundreds of bullets whistling into the haystack.

To a "Crash!" "Crash!" "Crash!' "Crash!" Watt peeped out, and frowned.

"The end of our poor old plane?" inquired the Observer.

"Yes," answered Watt soberly. "They've turned a battery on to it. They've just about got the range now. Yes, there she goes!"

And up went the plane in a scurry of smoke with fragments of twisted metal.

Watt sighed.

Then – "Crash!" Right close by. Watt whistled. The Observer sighed.

"Crash!" "Crash!" "Crash!"

"This nice, comfortable haystack will burn merrily," remarked the Observer lastly.

"Yes, but if you think you are just going to lie here and dodge that hiding then you are very much mistaken," replied Watt. "How do you feel now."

"I could almost fight you," smiled the Observer.

"Very well. Come and let us do it."

And up they went in the air.

'I'his time, it was the Observer who pulled Watt from the blazing haystack. Half blinded by smoke, with shells now bursting close around them they staggered away towards the French lines, running when their lungs were clear of smoke.

And now it was the smoke that saved them. In a furious crescendo of machine gun and rifle fire they ran in smoke which, blown by the wind, was streaming out towards the French front line.

This volume of smoke from the blazing stack was a screen

through which the German gunners could only mistily see glimpses of the running men.

They tumbled down into the French trenches with a wild cheer ringing in their ears.

The Observer lay there gasping. It had been a long run, a terrible run for him.

"The Legion – always does it," he smiled. "1 apologize - for asking you – to run away – from me."

They smiled and shook hands – the grip of the Legion.

10

TRAINING THE YOUNG WAR BIRDS

The men of the Legion earned their honours hard. And the Australian Legionaire, Soldat Watt, earned three honours. The Legion d' Honneur, the Croix de Guerre, and the rank of brevet Capitaine.

Then came 1916. And the Australian Flying Corps.

The Australian Legionaire was wild with delight. To think that far away Australia unknown to the world until Anzac would now take her place in the flying battles of the Nations. There was only one body of men in all the world he would rather be among than in the Legion, and that was in the Australian Flying Corp.

The Legion just hated losing him, he was one of them. But now Australia and France were one.

"He is still one of us," frowned the Legion, "and it is but natural that the young eagle should fly with his own home brood. But we hate to lose him."

So brevet-Capitaine Watt was transferred to the Australian Flying Corps. With his great experience he was promptly made Captain Oswald Watt, Flight Commander in command of No. 2 Squadron.

They trained in England. And No. 2 Squadron took to Watt as the Legion had taken to him, no one could help liking the man. And he put them through their paces, flew the Squadron from its English base to St. Omer in France in one day. No British Squadron had yet done that. Such a short trip seems laughable when we remember the world travelling

Group portrait of Lieutenant Colonel (Lt Col) Watt and officers of the 68th Squadron, Australian Flying Corps, at Baizieux, after the fighting at Cambrai. Left to right, back row: Lieutenant (Lt) L. F. Loder; Lt T. Grant; Captain (Capt) L. H. Holden MC; Capt R. W. Howard MC; Lt L. Benjamin; Capt W. A. Robertson; Lt A. Pratt. Front row: Lt C. C. Sands; Lt H. Taylor MC MM; Lt L. S. Truscott; Lt F. A. Power (partially obscured); Lt P. H. Lawson; Lt D. C. Allardice; Capt H. G. Forrest DFC; Lt Col W. O. Watt OBE; Lt L. R. Clark; Capt G. C. Wilson MC DCM. Kneeling: Lt W. A. Turner; Capt F. G. Huxley MC machines of today. But in 1916-17 the speed and reliability of the aeroplanes was far less than it is today.

Under the leadership of Commander Oswald Watt the 2nd Squadron soon became famous, its deeds are imperishably carried in the annals of flying warfare. But Major Watt now in command of a Squadron could no longer fly to battle. His job was now that of the planner, the lives of his Squadron lay in his mind. Let him make but one mistake - .

He could not rest when his Patrols were out, not until his young flying men were safe home again. We sing a very popular song now "Put me to bed Sargent-Major!"Well, Oswald Watt was that first Sarn-major.

He was the guardian of his officers and men, not only did he plan their battles but he looked after their health and comfort day and night. He insisted that his flying officers go to bed early, and that they be not called unless absolutely necessary. When the Squadron were in action there was no rest for him and none until hours after they had returned and been tucked safely away to bed. One of many days he was fearfully worried, a young officer had failed to return on time. Watt could not rest. Fourteen hours later they bought him a wire, the lad had crashed but was safe. Watt threw his cap in the air and danced with joy. Then they led him away to sleep.

He was now a rich man, but he lived as simply as his youngest officer. When money was forwarded him he used it among them all, they all shared together. When it was done they lived as poor soldiers - until the next cheque came.

But perhaps these written words of an officer who lived and fought under him will tell you more of the man.

"He possessed every quality to make him a great leader of men. Courage, determination, an immense capacity for work, a stern and just sense of discipline, unfailing courtesy and thoughtfulness for all his subordinates, and above all that greatest factor in leadership, a genius for

On the ground at Toul, March 17 1916, in front of Watt's MF 11*bis,* which he named The Kangaroo.

endearing himself, without conscious effort, to all who enjoyed the privilege of serving under him. Only too many of us found in him a friend such as we had never found before, and such as we shall never find again. "

And that was what his own Australian men thought of him. No wonder the Legion had loved him.

In 1918 he was promoted to Lieutenant-Colonel and was sent to England to command the Australian Training Wing. It was now very near the Armistance but no one knew that then. Watt immediately set himself the task of training these Australian lads for the stern job ahead. What a joy-loving, heedless, skylarking crowd they were. Firmly but kindly Watt started the training that was to turn these lads into cool, quick-thinking men who would prove terrible fighters while yet guarding their own lives.

The Australian Training Wing was situated in the heart of a fox hunting country where fox hunting for centuries has been not only a sport, but a solemn rite. One day a great hunt was in full swing over the sunlit English countryside. The blowing of the horn, the mustering of the hounds, the red coats, the lords and ladies on their beautiful horses. "Tallyho!" and the fox was away.

Three young Australian pilots joined in the hunt – from the air. They thought it was glorious fun. They zoomed down with a roar cheering on the fox. What catastrophe! horses bolted in all directions flying hedges leaping ditches galloping madly for the wide-open spaces. The hounds scattered terrified, tails between their legs. In shrieking delight those mad Australians carried on with the hunt in which only themselves and the fox was left. That fox had the race of his life with three roaring aeroplanes swooping at his tail, leaping hedges and roads to zoom down over the fields with wheels almost touching the earth. And didn't that fox travel! I'll say he did! They chased him right into his hole, he vanished like a scalded cat.

Then the pilots looped the loop to the amazement of the yokels, flew low over a village street and blew kisses to the girls then joy rode home to tell the great hunt to the mess.

Oh, but what a row. The hunting people were frightfully angry. Such a thing, had never, never, happened before. One of the Heads was a Duke and what he didn't say on paper against the Australian pilots was just. too bad. He dispatched that fearsome letter post haste to the Air Ministry. And the Air Ministry, in turn, wrote a terrible letter to the O.C. of the Australian Training Wing. That letter demanded the names of the culprits, and sundry reprisals to be done to them.

Colonel Watt smiled, then his face grew grim. He knew this was no joke. The lads really had been at fault, a serious fault too but after all they had not understood.

The Colonel shielded his men, refused to give their names. Instead, he went to the Duke. At first his Grace was unbending. But Colonel Watt was very patient, very understanding. He knew that the Duke and his friends had a very just cause of complaint, but he wanted them to realize the Australian side of the question also. And as quietly he admitted the justice of the complaint so the Duke began to listen. And presently was completely won over by the charm of the Australian officer. They ended up by shaking hands and enjoying a good laugh over it. Then sat down to a pleasant dinner together.

The Duke withdrew his letter of complaint. The Air Ministry lost its ferocity. Thus the young offenders, like the fox; escaped with a whole skin.

But they almost wished they had not escaped. They were ordered to toe the mat before the Colonel and the dressing down he gave them they had not forgotten to this day.

Thereafter, no one from the Wing joined in a fox hunt - not in an aeroplane.

After the war, Colonel Oswald Watt, one time Soldat Watt of the Legion returned to Australia. But his heart was still in the sir and with the men he had commanded. He found himself a wealthy man now, he helped his war birds to employment, helped them in many ways. As President of the New South Wales Aero Club, and in other activities he did great work for civil Aviation.

Big business interests soon chained him to the city. But he still loved the bush. He seldom could get right away but he had a lovely weekend camp at Bilgola, on the coast north of Manly. Here it was his delight to relax with axe and spade in garden and bush. He loved too the surf on the pretty little beach.

One morning, he went for a swim. He never came back.

Viva! Soldat of the Legion.

Watt and crew in winter kit, France 1916.

11

THE JUBILEE MAIL

"BILL" Taylor saw his eighteenth birthday in 1915 and celebrated it by donning the Aussie uniform. He was a footslogger. But he wanted to fly. He did. ln 1917. As 2nd Lieutenant P.C. Taylor of the R.F.C.. Roaring across to France with 60th Squadron, a fighting crowd of dare-devils manhandling Sopwith Pups.

And then - Bill was the leader of a patrol roaring out over the German lines looking for fight. He got. it. From the depths or a cloud the Huns dived with motors full out as bombs crashed, with the machines screaming down, their guns spitting death. Bill picked his victim and the Hun met him in a vicious swoop with guns blazing. Then Bill and his Patrol and the Huns were all mixed up in a roaring whirlwind of death.

Bill saw his Hun screech down in a trail of smoke, Bill side-slipped, then dived only to roar up again as two Huns closed on· him while he sped for the tail of another to suddenly realise the enemy was powerfully reinforced, the Patrol had run into a trap, the air was alive with Huns.

It was a fight to the death then with those that were cornered while the wounded ones sped to hide in a cloud or planed far down in a desperate attempt to reach their own lines.

Lucky for young Bill Taylor that he was a cool and resourceful pilot though, facing almost certain death. Steadily working the controls

'Corporal Ellins (left), my rigger, and Corporal McFall, my mechanic, with me and Sopwith Scout 7309 at Vert Galant Farm, 1917.' Gordon Taylor.

19th Squadron, Chartles Kingsford Smith, without a cap in second row, right.

his brain was racing but very clearly as he twisted and turned and lodged in the midst of ten enemy machines roaring upon him from every angle, In the furious excitement of those terrible minutes there flashed before and around him and above and below charging machines and wings of machines and bellies of machines with upside down glimpses of leather-capped figures crouching over controls and machine guns.

Bill kept his head all through that furious half hour fight, completely cut off from his comrades. He fought his way towards home, swooped over the lines and landed.

His machine wits shot through and through.

"How on earth did you keep her in the air?" inquired the admiring mechanics.

"I hardly know," smiled Bill. "Everything was happening so quickly."

Well I'm blessed!" exclaimed a mechanic and stared.

The wire on his elevator, and the wire on the rudder had been shot through.

Bill Taylor should have crashed to earth.

But he had duplicated those wires before he took the air.

It was this forethought coupled with efficiency and grim determination that in the years to come was to make Bill Taylor famous in the story of world aviation.

The young Australian war bird was so popular that there was never lack of volunteers to go in his Patrols. He carried out forty, all offensive, always seeking fight. But before he left on patrol he always saw that his machine and those of his fighting mates was always in first class trim.

He became a tiger when they told him that brother Ken of the Royal Garrison Artillery had been killed in Belgium. The enemy learned to dread the avenging roar of his machine. From the misty skies his Patrols roared down blasting the enemy trenches with bombs, machine-gunning artillery though their planes wobbled in the crash of bursting shells. Bill Taylor's fiercest delight was to roar out over the German lines at the head of a flock of daredevils, soar up into the sky and climb up over the clouds then cruise far and wide seeking a. stronger force of Huns. They followed Bill's lead and dived straight down into them with a howl of machines that immediately broke up into hurricane dog fights that ended only when the surviving enemy turned tail and fled.

The daredevils of the air lived fast, fought faster, died with a laugh on their lips. No wonder when the chance came for fun they made the pace a cracker, too.

Captain Bill Taylor earned his promotion and decorations. Captain P.C. Taylor, M.C., in 1918 was transferred to the air fighting section of the Australian Flying Corps at Point Cook. It was a very big promotion.

Sorrowfully he said farewell to his war birds.

He arrived back in Australia just as the war ended.

But he stuck to flying, he loved it. Became pilot in the service of National Airways and there met Kingsford Smith and Ulm.

That meeting meant much to the lives of all three. They were to fly to fame together, the world was to acclaim them. They did not know it yet.

But each was an Ace in his own line. Thoroughly competent, brainy, and cool.

And each was a determined man, determined to do something great.

Taylor was now a first-class navigator. And such men were rare. Smith and Ulm were to prove two of the of the greatest pilots the world has known.

But all three were to battle hard in civilian life before fame came the way of each.

Very few men reach Fame without a heart-breaking struggle first.

In 1934 Smith and Taylor flew the *Southern Cross* to England. They planned the first east flight of the Pacific.

They did it. Seven thousand three hundred and fifty water miles never before flown by a single-engined plane. Overnight they became front page news.

Taylor was far-seeing. Over that vast expanse of the Pacific he had noted many an island, little tiny pin-points every here and there away down in the ocean.

Those islands would make great hopping off places, he thought.

Stages across both the Tasman and the Pacific from which aeroplanes could fly to and from the old world to Australia and. New Zealand. As landing grounds and refueling stations they would make possible the great commercial air routes that he visioned in the future. And they were priceless for the defence of the Pacific, and of the far-flung Empire.

He placed his views before the Authorities. But to no avail. They did not think that world events were moving so fast.

Time has since proved that events and nations have moved fast indeed since aeroplanes conquered the skies.

Taylor was destined to fly and navigate in some of the greatest flights in aviation history. But perhaps his most thrilling, more thrilling even aerial dogfight against many foes was the flight across the Tasman with the Jubilee Mail.

The famous "Smithy" as pilot, "Bill" Taylor as navigator, John Stannage as wireless man.

The big day came. Midnight. The *Southern Cross* lay dreaming. Phantom lights. Shadowy mechanics. Aviators drawing on leather coats, goggles, caps. Tang of the quiet night.

Subdued murmur of voices. Silent machines, squat machines, silent propellors facing skyward. Smithy started the motors. Life awakened in the *Southern Cross*.

It roared in a rapid crescendo, throbbing to reach to the stars   They climbed aboard. Taylor by, Smithy in the starboard pilot's seat, Stannage with his mystic wireless gadgets aft.

She faced the night with a threatening roar, she trembled through and through. She took to the air. She was away. Alone in the sky. Fleecy clouds like ghostly bridal veils. Up she climbed, into the silent world of stars.

She slips out over the ghostly land and is above the whispering sea. Hum of motors, smell of oil, feeble light. Smithy's magic touch at the controls, his humorous, weather-lined face quizzing the gadgets faintly illuminated.

Taylor at the map, the navigating instruments. Stannage with phones to his ear, wireless rapping out messages carried on the air waves of space.

The stars. Cold air. The sea. A speck of human-made mechanism speeding through space.

A hundred miles out, over the lnvisible sea. And the mechanical speck speed under a floating cloud like a wisp of the night floating under a verandah. A hand drops a flare. It leaps up out of the sea, flares as a glowing point of light, swiftly dies astern.

A human gnome aloft frowns. He judges they are being set to the north at an angle which. he judges to be 8 degrees. So he lays off against this drift on the compass.

The steady throb. Three humans in a cabin far up .in the sky. The night. Space. And the sea.

Clouds gathered, spread, groped together, enclosed the machine. The clouds spat rain. Hours droned by. Other clouds enfolded the machine, draping her wings with vapour. She glided through, unseen. The pilot called Smithy took her blind through many clouds, holding her three thousand feet above the sea.

What gave him the brains. The feeling. The knowledge to do this. He was but a man. They say that Man developed from a protoplasm, a jellyfish of the sea. The three motors roared steadily. The three propellers a whirling gleam in cloud and mist and rain.

At five in the morning Taylor gave Smithy a spell at the flying. They grinned at one another. The old bus was going sweetly. Smithy crawled aft to Stannage to send some flying messages. For, you see, these descendants of Jellyfish had developed the power to send messages through the air. Truly if the scientists be right, we have developed amazingly since our ancestors were jellyfish.

Smithy's good-humoured face did not look that of a protoplasm as he grinned at Stannage.

Stannage grinned back, he looked to be a good-humoured man with no appetite. They flashed out a message through space to the Australian land where in a second it was received, hundreds of miles away.

Steady hum of the motors. Cold of the coming dawn. The mechanical speck flitting onward thousands of feet above the invisible sea.

At the controls Taylor peered into cloud and driving rain. The throb of the machine was a living thing, the warmth of its heart was his shelter and comfort. Taylor peered from the starboard seat over the top side of the centre motor. Through the darkness he saw a flame, just like a dancing will-o'-th'-wisp.

He eyed it curiously, it really was the heated exhaust manifold glowing brightly, At last it occurred to him that a spot on top of the exhaust manifold on the starboard side of the motor was glowing with a lighter, brighter colour than the rest of the visible portion of the exhaust ring.

He frowned This should not be.

The speck flies on. Invisible in mist and cloud and rain. A big cloud ahead. They plunge into it and faintly it melts away from them as a ghost might edge away from a clutching hand. Everything lightens. Dawns is up over the sea far away ahead. Dawn has come. Old Sol is rising up to see what he can see. The nose of the machine takes shape. A beam from Sol kisses the tip.

Suddenly a flame appears on the manifold. It dims, narrows to a fine slit, glows to a jumping, flickering threat of light. Taylor's eyes grow wide, his heart misses a beat.

The welded edge of the exhaust manifold is being carried away before his staring eyes.

The crack was creeping up and over behind the top of the cylinder. The metal began to give way. The exhaust blew out. Soon, the top of the manifold would carry away.

The machine would fritter away in pieces, in space above the sea.

Smithy returned to the cockpit. Grinned. Settled down at the controls. Taylor pointed. As they stared, the rapidly breaking pipe bulged, flickered into the airstream - was gone.

Terrific vibration shook the *Southern Cross*, as if some titanic hand had grasped and was shaking the life out of her. The starboard motor leaped and struggled like a bolting horse. A sickly, pulsing wobble tore through the fuselage as Smithy shut down the starboard motor the hauled the *Cross* up almost on her tail. He opened out the other two motors to full throttle.

Dawn burst through the sky, lit up the rolling sea.

As Smithy almost stalled the engine an ominous quietness filled the cabin, the terrible vibrations slowed down while still the airstream turned the slowing propeller. They stared as it slowly came to rest with the splintered blade pointing like a finger of doom.

Grimly Smithy turned the stricken *Cross* and headed her back towards the Australian coast.

All their hopes, all their careful plans completely wrecked. Lucky indeed should they escape with their lives. This meant ruin to what had

The *Southern Cross*, with Smithy at the controls, 1934.

John Stannage, "Smithy" and "Bill" Taylor, 1935.

promised to be a very fine accomplishment. They hardly dared glance at one another. Sick at heart they sat and stared as the weakening plane turned slowly back.

Smithy held her nose up to the skies and now came the test of the super-pilot, the eagle of the air on broken wing fighting death, fighting with every nerve to keep height! Height! Height!

With full throttle on the two remaining motors the altimeter needle slowly crept down, down.

She already was losing height, losing height.

"We must dump something," shouted Taylor.

Through the roar of the motors Smithy's voice came faintly back. "Anything! Except th' mail!"

Taylor hurried below to the cabin.

"Overboard with everything heavy," he shouted. "Quick! Everything except th' mail!"

Stannage snatched at the luggage, out went the first case through the cabin door.

Taylor hurried back to turn the drain-cock on the main cabin tank.

For they must even dump their fuel while being extremely careful to leave enough to reach the coast.

Smithy was fighting at the controls, nursing her, nursing her. Slowly, slowly she was losing height. Through drifting clouds sunlight in feeble spurts now glinted on the cold sea below.

Five hundred and ninety miles out to sea. A broken propeller, one engine konked out, the Cross balanced as on a hair; again and again they held their breaths as she shuddered to stall.

But again and again Smithy's cunning fingers pulled her back from the fatal dive.

With feverish mind but terribly cool reasoning Taylor calculated to the ounce just how much petrol he might safely dump.

Calculated the speed of the machine, that terrible distance between them and land, the number of hours flying necessary to get there, the gallons of petrol the motors would need. Their lives depended on Smithy. And again their lives depended on the correctness of that petrol calculation.

Slowly, very slowly, she kept on losing height. Taylor turned the drain cock and the life-blood of the *Southern Cross* began draining away to sea.

Stannage had hurled the luggage, equipment, tools, all out the cabin door. The bags of precious mail in piles lay lashed in the cabin with ropes.

In the old days of the horse mail, the camel mail and the coach mail throughout every disaster the driver always franticly clung to the mails.

Save the Mails!

And now – the hard-pressed eagles of the air tried to save the mails.

The Jubilee Mail.

1 2

MEN WHO NEVER GIVE IN

TAYLOR hurried to the pilots' cabin.

"Everything's well in hand down below!" he shouted.

They glanced at one another. Smiled. Turned to their fight again.

The altimeter showed only five hundred feet. She had come down very near the sea.

"That lightening of the load. has eased her," said Smithy. "I'm just about holding her now. She'll do it if the motor can stand up to full throttle."

Meanwhile upon distant Australia and New Zealand there burst this lone drama of the air, speeding out through space as Stannage stuck grimly to the wireless.

To Sydney.

7.a.m. "Propeller smashed on starboard motor. Please inform all stations stand by. May not be able to hold height."

7.1 a.m. "Turned back. Please stand by for position and course. Bill is busy. Please tell all ships to stand by on 600 metres."

7.2 a.m. "Am going to dump heavy things, and gas also."

7. 7 a.m. "Have to dump the lot I think. Can' t keep height. Hope they have a fast destroyer at Garden Island. What a hard end for the old *Cross*."

7 .5 a.m. "Looks like we are going in. Gee, it's cold! Of course it

would happen when we are right in the middle of it. Wonder what splintered the propeller. Might have been a dicky bird, but unlikely. Smithy says not to dump the mails."

7.21 a.m. "Heavens. One of the other engines spluttered."

Hour after hour as the flight went on so the messages came hurtling through space. Australia. and New Zealand listened breathlessly.

Smithy at the controls was holding her in the air with hands and feet, coaxing her as a champion rider would a hurt and touchy horse. *The Cross* roaring hoarsely forward felt to be leaning in the air, sometimes she staggered but kept plunging on, just, staying there. Smithy was feeling her through his hands and feet and mind, feeling just where her strength lay and utilizing it, nursing it to push her on, shielding her weakness all he humanly could. With his man-given genius and what remained of her strength he was working to win support for her stricken body from the slowed up air stream, at the magic of His touch she laid her wings upon it at exactly the one and only angle which she could still fly and keep height. Should he make but one slip she would roar her battling way down to the sea hopelessly beaten against the odds of weight and loss of power. But she battled on to the touch of the man, hour after nervy hour. The harsh crackling coming from the two remaining motors reminded Taylor of the snarl of a cornered beast roaring defiance.

"Good old *Cross!*" he whispered, "keep your nose into it old girl. Just keep on going."

Stannage came smiling with a message received through the air from A.W.A.

"All extremely sorry hear your unfortunate experience. Everything possible being done. Everyone hoping the old bus holds out."

And again.

From Headquarters, Sydney.

"Pilot boat *Captain Cook* has left, intercepting your course given at 10 47.

H,M.S. *Sussex* will be ready to leave in three hours if you fail to reach the coast.

Faith in Australia approved given for use. Now endevouring locate pilot. Will be dispatched on your course soon as possible. Please radio instructions.

They grinned cheerfully, they were not entirely alone in the world.

Each turned back to his job.

Hours went by. Patches of sunlight lit up the sea. They were now three hundred and thirty miles from land, they might even reach that land.

And then Taylor noticed a faint trail of blue smoke blowing from the port exhaust.

The port motor was burning oil!

The terrible significance of it burst upon them. If they could not get oil to the hot motor it would burn itself out and they must plunge into the sea.

The irony of it. The working motor shrieking for oil., a tank full of oil by the useless starboard motor.

If only there was some means of getting this oil and feeding it into the motor

Screeching for it.

But the starboard oil tank was away out on the fuselage under the howling Wind.

 Perhaps everything would be all right.

Taylor went forward to starboard seat beside Smithy to give him a spell. He put his feet to the rudder bar and took the rudder bar and took the wheel in his hands. Immediately he felt the battle of the screaming air against the staggered machine.

For five hours Smithy had sat there, fighting a terrible battle.

Taylor glanced at the port oil-pressure gauge. It showed steady at 63 pounds to the square inch. He sighed in great relief. Everything was all right. He flew a while, then glanced at the gauge. And the blood seemed to freeze in his veins.

The gauge was flickering. Fascinated he watched it. That tiny needle was the register of death.

It was falling.

His eyes sought Smithy. Smithy's tired face turned to the gauge. Smithy's eyes narrowed, the lines came deep in his face as he frowned.

He took over and throttled back the port motor, gave it several bursts. Then opened it all out again.

The pressure lay just below sixty pounds.

He smiled at Taylor, shrugged his shoulders.

The needle quivered ever so slightly, then slipped down a wee bit.

Very soon, the pressure was down to 50 lb. It wouldn't be long now. The motor would crack to pieces and they would fall down to the waiting sea.

Taylor went down to the cabin. Stannage, busy at the wireless, looked up questioningly. Then shrugged with a smile. And rapped out this message.

"Port motor will only last quarter of an hour. Please stand by tor exact position."

And the world waited. There was nothing more to be done. Taylor crawled back to the cockpit. Smithy was taking off his boots. He grinned. Good old Smithy, he would fight to the very last.

The pressure was down to 55 lb.

Taylor was staring, listening.

"Get the oil from the starboard tank, quickly. Get it! Get it!"

Was it a Voice? imagination? What?

He hurried to the cabin, slung off his shoes, belted his coat tightly around him, snatched a light line and slipped back to the cockpit.

"Going to have a try at getting some oil;" he shouted.

Smithy turned his face with a cheery smile that said "Good old boy." But he shook his head. The attempt meant death. They might as well all go together.

"I'm going to give it a try!" shouted Taylor determinedly.

He lashed the line around his waist, tied the other end in the cockpit, stood on the starboard seat and flung a leg over the side. The air stream snatched his leg like the clutch from a gigantic hand, howling at him the futility of the attempt.

He pressed down his leg, groping for the streamlined tube which runs out along the fuselage, he got his toe on to the strut and sensed space below his heel. Smithy was watching, feet and hands on the controls. The port motor was roaring maddeningly, with burnt smoke in a long trail now pouring from the exhaust. The sea was coming closer, there were eager waves upon it, leaping up at them.

Taylor firmly grasped the cockpit edge then slung over the other leg and was standing on the tube as a driven mouse might crawl along a guttering. Pressed flat by the wind. He gasped as the breath was whipped from his lungs, the wind screamed around his face, it pushed him with terrible force.

His fingers felt like pulsing steel gripping the cockpit edge.

My God! If he slipped!

With shoulders braced against the edge of the wing he clung and fought panic. The screaming wind would blow his eyes out if he looked ahead. With clenched teeth, face all screwed up, shoulders hard against the wing, he clung there with a death-grip to the edge of the cockpit.

Panic passed, seemed to scream away with the wind. A heavenly

Smithy and Stannage.

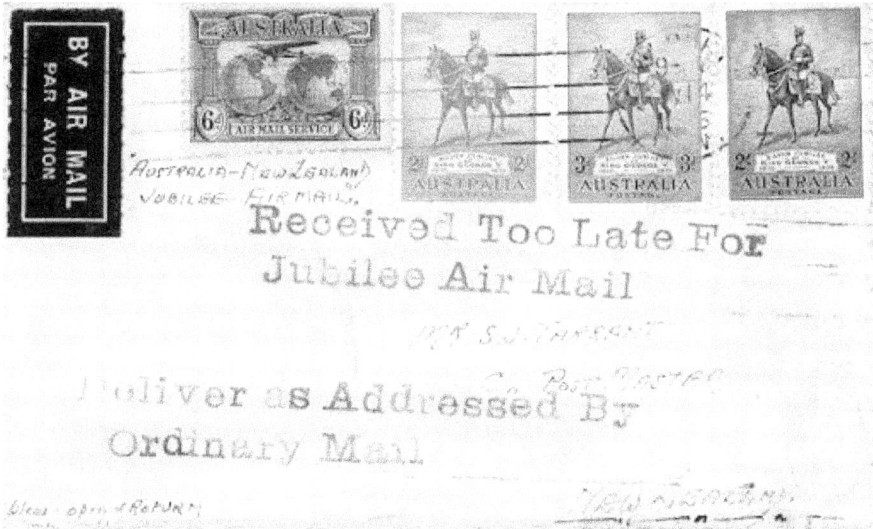

feeling of confidence came as morphia numbs pain so died the feeling that he would be swept out into space.

He let go with his right hand and stretched out towards the engine. He edged his feet inch by inch along the strut while clinging to the cockpit edge with his left hand. Bracing his shoulders bard against the wing he edged out – out – out.

He could not reach the engine and still grip the cockpit. He must let go his grip of the cockpit. He fought for a long, long breath.

Stannage, white of face, was staring from the plane.

Taylor pressed hos shoulders against the wing, felt his toes gripping into the strut, then let go his hold of the cockpit.

Instantly he wanted to fling out his arms to the engine but instantly too icy caution whispered "Consolidate your position here against wing and strut! Then shuffle out steady inch by inch and cautiously reach the motor!"

He obeyed. And grasped the engine mounting.

Sudden panic. He would never be able to return!

Again, panic fled with the shrieking wind.

He hooked his left arm around a strut and bent over the cowl, his fingers working at the cowl pins. The first pin stuck, he forced the strength or steel into his fingers and at last pulled out the pin. The other pins came easily. He wrenched the side cowl free to get at the drain-plug.

A spanner?

Stannage was leaning far out, a spanner in hand. Taylor clung to the engine, shuffled back along the strut, reached out his left arm and just reached the spanner. He shuffled back.

Smithy was handling the machine as he never, never had handled a machine before. A broken machine, slowly, losing height. A man far away out there, away out there in the wind.

Taylor struggled to straddle then sit and keep sitting on the horizontal strut that leads out from the fuselage to just below the oil tank. He hooked his arm around a steel tube and began tightening the spanner on to the head of the drain-plug. He looked like a birds-nest far out on the branch of a storm-tossed tree.

The plug unscrewed to the spanner.

But he had nothing to put the oil in.

He gazed around. Stannage was back there, holding up a thermos flask.

Taylor shuffled back, gripped the flask, and came back along the strut again. He hooked his left arm around a tube, unscrewed the plug, filled the cannister with oil. Screwed back the plug.

And now to get back. With only one hand free!

He did it. As he passed the tin to Stannage the flying suction of the slipstream whipped half the oil away.

Stannage emptied the oil into a container and passed back the flask. Again Taylor edged out for oil. Again, and yet again.

When he climbed back into the cockpit he just wanted to lie down there, close his eyes, and gasp.

But the oil-pressure gauge – it was down to the very last gasp.

That oil must be put in the port engine, away out on the other wing! Quickly!

They were almost down to the sea.

Taylor climbed around Smithy and put his leg over the side. He fought place his foot on the port side strut, then forced his body partly out.

A howling blast hurled him against the bulkhead. He crouched there breathlessly. Maddened by failure he thought of nothing but of getting that oil into the port engine, he forgot he must now fight against the slipstream between the two working motors. He pushed out into the roaring flood of wind and again was hurled back into the cockpit.

Beaten and breathless he stared into Smithy's eyes and those eyes spoke. Smithy's right hand went the throttle and pushed them right open as Taylor stared, now realizing what Smithy was doing. Hauling and coaxing and Willing and lifting the *Cross* up, lifting her for height with the very last gasp now in her.

Labouringly she responded, trying hard, hard. Seven hundred feet was her utmost limit. Smithy nodded, and shut down the port motor. Taylor went over the side, the one remaining motor roaring with a terrible labouring strain as it struggled to hold up the engine. But now, with only one motor running the force of the slipstream was lessened by half. Taylor felt he could just fight against the wind. He must be quick and sure for now with only one motor the *Cross* must lose height fast.

He slithered out to the port motor and draped himself over the cowl, just in time, the waves were licking up, spray struck the machine. Smithy now opened up the port motor, she roared, picked up, began to climb.

The *Cross* had almost touched the surface of the sea. Taylor clung there watching the waves so close as Smithy and the *Cross* fought again to regain height. With his head well down Taylor clung against the roar of the straining motors at full throttle. The drive of the air from the propellor seemed to suck the very air from his clinging body.

Smithy climbed high as he could. Then shut down the port motor. Feverishly then Taylor got to work on the top cowl over the filler cap of the oil tank. He emptied that oil into the oil tank.

Moments of awful suspense.

Then – gleeful faces, shouts and waving from the cockpit.

The oil-pressure gauge was creeping up.

Taylor buried his face in his arms and laughed, laughed down at the angry sea.

Smithy signalled. Taylor lay over the cowl again, clinging tight. The motor came on with a booming roar. Again the *Cross* began to roar up from the sea. Taylor clung, waiting for height so that he could again pour more oil into the tank.

As he clung, he felt a mad feeling of exhilaration, success had come and he was flying through open air with the teeth of a million demons whistling in his ears. But they would never, never pluck him away.

Again and again he crawled out to feed the port motor with oil. The motor gasped its last when they were almost over the coast. They made the landing.

Mechanic Tom Pethybridge removing the broken propeller on the *Southern Cross* upon safely landing the Jubilee Mail. *Below:* Smithy.

13

THE "FLYING WRECK"

"£10,000 waiting at the end of the rainbow," said Ray Parer slowly, "and we haven't a shilling in the world!" He grinned rueully at his companion.

Lieutenant J.C. McIntosh nodded sympathetically, then turned out his pockets.

"Empty as our heads," he laughed.

"Be blowed to that!" declared Parer suddenly. "We'll do it! We'll fly to Australia if we have to grow our own wings!"

"1'm with you!" swore McIntosh. And the dare-devil mates shook hands.

Truly they were up against it. It was in England, at the end of the Great War. The Australian Government had just offered a prize of £10,000 to the first men who could fly from England to Australia. A breath-taking job, in those days of the clumsy old "flying crates." But many ambitious Australian war aces were wild to try their luck - for the honour and the prize.

By the end of November every competitor but one who could secure a machine, had already flown on the first stage to the great prize. Parer and McIntosh were still battling all over Great Britain for a plane. At last they were introduced to Lord Dewar.

"You certainly are triers," he said.

"We're going to try until we get there." replied Parer grimly. "Only give us a machine, any sort or machine."

"Sit down and we'll talk it over," invited his lordship. "What's yours?" he asked.

"Dewar's," answered McIntosh promptly. Lord Dewar smiled:

"We're along famously." Then, after a pause: "There are only two things I'll ask of you. Win the prize if you possibly can and - deliver a present of Dewar's to a very old friend of mine in Australia."

With glasses half way to their lips they stopped, wild-eyed.

"You don't mean it?" whispered Parer in the sudden silence.

Lord Dewar nodded. "I like men with courage," he said. "I'll back you."

"To Dewar's!" shouted McIntosh and they toasted the grand adventure.

With the cheque given them by Lord Dewar they hurried to a great Government sale of second-hand war material. It was a thrilling moment - and they bought a De Havilland 9, a bi-plane with two cockpits, a little bit the worse for wear.

"She's a bit of an old warhorse," chuckled Parer, "but she'll do us."

"She's the best machine ever built," declared McIntosh. "We'll fly around the world in her."

Lovingly they examined the engine, a 240 h.p. Siddeley Puma.

"There's a nut or two missing," mused Parer. "Seems to be cracked cylinder somewhere or other too. But we'll soon tinker that up."

"A bit of straining wire here and there and a spot of paint on her tail will work wonders," answered McIntosh confidently.

The machine had been designed and built as a long-range bomber – though "long-range" did not mean very far in those days.

"She's built for endurance and distance anyway," declared Parer at last.

"She's a brave old scout. And just look at the old joystick! I'll bet it's given many a thrill to some fine lad."

They gazed silently, knowing what that joystick had meant to the touch of the pilot fighting for his life in the air. Parer sighed. Then, briskly:

"Well, she's a wonderful machine. We'll make her ship-shape, then start off. The others must be half way across the globe by now."

"We'll catch them up, all right," declared McIntosh. We could do anything in this bonny machine."

But the authorities did not think it was a wonderful machine.

"We forbid you authority to fly," they declared. "That machine is utterly unsuitable for such a great flight. We forbid you to take the air."

Parer looked at McIntosh, McIntosh looked at Parer. McIntosh winked, Parer winked.

And one morning the birds had flown.

One of the greatest flights of history, 12,000 miles in a worn-out plane... And the race was lost when they started, for Ross Smith and his crew had got a long start and they won the prize - they earned it too.

None of the other planes got through - except the Flying Wreck. Into the teeth of a howling gale with the old "wreck" screeching in every joint, tossed through scudding clouds and pelting rain with crashing thunder that drowned the moan of the tortured engine. Ray Parer, the wonder navigator, with eyes red-rimmed from the strain, his hand frozen to the joystick. McIntosh crouched there sending out his indomitable spirit and matchless courage to the men whose hand and heart and mind were holding their battered machine together as they hurtled through the storm.

After several hundred turbulent miles they were forced down in France and were marooned there for a fretful month. A great day

Parer and McIntosh with their De Havilland 9, ready to go.

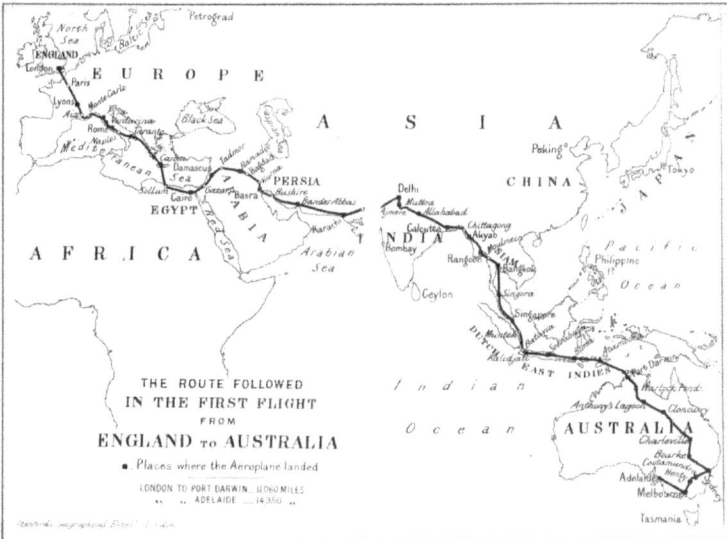

Ross Smith's plan of the winning flight to Australia.

came when, to a cheering crowd, the Flying Wreck roared into the air again bound for the cities of Italy.

And by a hairs-breadth the two men escaped a terrible death. The massive crater of Vesuvius loomed up, a black thundercloud lazily rolling far up from the mighty volcano McIntosh leaned to Parer, making signs and trying to shout above the roar of the engine.

"I wonder what the old fire looks like from above?"

"We'll see!" bawled Parer and jerked down his thumb to Mcintosh's nod as the Flying Wreck soared up, up, up to just below the black cloud and, wheeling like an eagle, soared over the mighty furnace. They gazed down, overawed as they peered into that molten lake boiling in the bowels of the crater. Smoke dimmed their eyes, sulphur fumes choked their nostrils as they gazed down into the dull red glow. Parer tilted the joystick, and down they dived as if right into the fiery pit. Suddenly Parer wrenched at the joystick - the plane was clutched by a fierce downward draught as if by a demon's hand. Parer worked frantically.

McIntosh held his horrified breath as the draught sucked them down, down. Right at the lip of the crater Parer regained control and the plane slipped side-ways, then zoomed up out of the clouds and just skimmed over the crater rim.

The two airmen soon landed. They were very shaken.

They started out again, over the blue Mediterranean with its wonder islands specked like tiny worlds in the lovely Aegean far below. A storm came in a lightning flash with crash of thunder that dually rocked the plane, a shrieking gust of wind almost sucked them from the cockpit - and away went their maps.

Tragedy. In those days aeronautical maps were rare indeed, and very expensive. And here they were near the borders of Turkey with their precious maps gone, the maps that were to have guided them to the other end of the world.

They landed. In a foreign country, distant from a city, too.

"Well, " said Parer ruefully, "we've got very little money, but we certainly do get some fun."

"Twig all those funny looking people hurrying along to the show," said McIntosh. "They think we've come down in a storm."

"If we open our mouths," grinned Parer, "they'll understand we want something to eat."

"I wish Lord Dewar was among them," answered McIntosh, "he wouldn't need a hint."

They could secure no flying maps, so they bought railway maps! "Fancy finding your way to Australia with a railway map printed in Turkey and Italy," said Parer. "No wonder the newspaper man think we're cracked."

"We're cracked in the right place, anyway," answered McIntosh energetically.

"And we're going to fly to Australia, map or no map."

"Sure - but we'll have to mend a crack in the old plane first. She's a beauty, she' s standing up to her job wonderfully."

"Well, so far the air hasn't been able to beat us," said McIntosh. "Two seas haven't been able to drown us, two storms haven't been able to down us, and a volcano hasn't been able to burn us."

Parer grinned. "We'll see what the desert can do then. But first see if we can get some dop from those yokels to plug up the leaks in this petrol pipe."

When high above the great Iraq desert, the old engine coughed, coughed again then sputtered warningly. Above them stretched a brilliant dome of sky, a blazing sun. Below, far as the eye could reach, was one vast brown sea of sand.

"Water?" they were both thinking. "Will there be water?" Again the engine groaned, spluttered, coughed despairingly. Then a great silence enveloped them as they began to glide down. Swiftly

2nd Lietenant Ray Parer, Australian Flying Corp.

the parched desert rose up to meet them.

They landed safely, stepped out and gazed around.

"We must be somewhere near the Garden of Eden."

"Looks like it," answered McIntosh cheerily, "so long as you imagine the roses and things. Baghdad lies only a few hundred miles ahead, isn't it in Mesopotamia somewhere or other that the Garden is supposed to grow?"

"Somewhere thereabouts," grinned Parer, "when Adam and Eve were boys and girls. But let's patch up the old engine or we'll do a perish from thirst."

Their brows streaming perspiration in that blazing heat, they worked busily for several hours until a hoarse shout made them jump around. Fierce Arabs on mangy camels had ridden right up to them. They stared at the bearded men clad in flowing burnous, nomads of the desert these, with the predatory eyes of hawks.

"I'll bet that hook-nosed robber on the bull camel has never had a wash in his life," said McIntosh.

"For heaven's sake smile," advised Parer, "they look like mischief. We're in a nasty fix."

He walked smilingly towards the Arabs, but the leader suddenly levelled his rifle.

With a warning cry, McIntosh whipped out a revolver. Arab and white man stared eye to eye in a deathly silence. Then Parer reached into the cockpit and turned around smiling, a revolver in one hand, a Mills bomb in the other. He showed them the bomb, then threw it up in the air, caught it again with a smile.

Then playfully made as if to throw it among the camelmen. With a hoarse cry of alarm they urged their camels apart.

"They know what Mills bombs mean," said McIntosh grimly. "You hurry on mending the plane while I keep these birds covered. Make a little pile of bombs handy to my feet. Then climb into the plane and gammon to fix a machine-gun, before you set to work on the engine."

All that afternoon Parer toiled at the engine while McIntosh stood guard.

The Arabs glowered from a little distance, almost on the point of starting an attack again and again. But fear of that supposed machine-gun held them back.

The adventurers took the air again at sundown laughing to a fusillade of parting shots. Two days later exactly the same adventure befell them. Yet again they bluffed their way through.

"It's a jolly queer thing," said Parer. "Twice now we've been forced down in a desert and right on top of a band of wandering cutthroats. And I suppose there's not another man within a hundred miles."

McIntosh frowned. "I didn't like the look of those long knives," he said. "But they'll never cut our throats; the good old crate won't let them."

"She certainly is a beauty," answered Parer enthusiastically, "she's holding together wonderfully."

The De Havilland 9 - when in action 1917.

14

TRIUMPH

THE Flying Wreck was holding together quite miraculously, but was becoming the worse for wear. She was squeaking and moaning in every joint, her tail was a bit out of plumb, a wing tip looked a bit skew-whiff, and they had their suspicions of the propeller. It was to take these two courageous men seven months to reach Australia, they were to battle through disasters and heart-burnings that would fill a book. They never would have won through had they not kept on smiling. With hardly any money left, they bad to do all their repairs themselves, had to find the materials for these.

"If only we were in the bush back in old Australia," sighed Parer again and again, "we could pull fencing wire off any Cocky's fence and patch up the old bus whenever we needed to."

"A strip or greenhide would certainly come in handy now," said McIntosh with a glance at the wobbly struts.

The two battlers accomplished wonderful things. Just to gift you an idea - Before they reached Australia they were forced to make or improvise, no less than five propellers. They practically rebuilt the Flying Wreck several times over.

They flew on to Baghdad and that city of the caliphs gave them a rousing reception.

"They must think we're Noah's Ark come to earth again,"

again," sighed McIntosh.

"Don't these people ever see people?"

"They don't see Australian airmen or the Flying Wreck every day," said Parer, with a grin.

It took them a hard fortnight's work in Baghdad to patch up the old Wreck; then she merrily took the air again. The adventurers circled the minarets and waved the old-time city a long farewell. With a wild "Hurrah!" to the skies, they set out for India.

They landed at Calcutta, still smiling. Parer pulled out his pockets.

McIntosh solemnly followed suit. The crowd gaped as if expecting to see the Mango Men emerge from those empty pockets.

"I know what we'll do," suggested Parer suddenly, "we'll raise the wind by giving joy-rides."

"Just the thing," laughed McIntosh, "and charge 'em double for the honour of going aloft in the Flying Wreck."

If only those Joy-riders had known! But they didn't. They paid eagerly for the privilege of riding in the Flying Wreck. This route had only been flown over once before. The innocents did not know what a risk they were taking.

"Ignorance is bliss," said McIntosh, grinning, as they counted their gains.

"The old Wreck still sticks to us," said Parer, "She's a fairy godmother, Actually a money-spinner. We'll never go broke again."

Up into blue skies again and then, with the engine konking out, they landed at Akyab on 1 April.

"A great day for joy-rides," said Parer. "I wonder who'll be the first?"

"We'd better knock that konk out of the engine first," warned McIntosh. "The old Wreck mightn't like us taking joy-rides aloft on All Fools Day!"

Parer nodded thoughtfully. "Perhaps you're right. Planes are touchy like humans sometimes."

Over plain and mountain, river and jungle they set out from Burma and the engine was a song in their ears. Never had the Flying Wreck behaved so sweetly - they felt, she could go on flying forever. They circled at Moulmein and came gliding down when, to Parer's horror, a great crowd of excited spectators appeared, rushing out on to the tiny landing ground. They must either crash into the crowd, or crash the machine. And with a cry that nearly meant tears Parer pulled on the joystick and crashed his beloved machine.

They crawled from the wreck. After the first shocked silence the crowd came rushing towards them. The two mates stood up and turned around to gaze at the machine.

Undercarriage and propeller were smashed, lower wing and radiator badly damaged. The Flying Wreck now looked a wreck indeed.

"I couldn't help it, old man," whispered Parer.

"Of course you couldn't," replied McIntosh huskily. "I'd never have forgiven you had you hurt any of those people. And the old bus wouldn't have forgiven you either."

Parer managed to smile. "We'll soon fix her up again."

"Of course we will."

And then, kindly people led them away to have their own injuries "fixed up."

Now began two months' constant thinking, hard work, perseverance and patience. These two men were cheery mates ever ready to help one another, with a laugh, with sympathy, with understanding. Otherwise, they could never have pulled through. Though one man's heart might sometime's be almost breaking, he would have a laugh and a joke to help the other along. So they laughed together, they battled together, and together they won out.

With great difficulty they managed to get a French propeller; it

The Flying Wreck, down but not out!

Needs a little bit of work...

was unsuitable, but they soon worked it into shape. Their radiator was smashed to pieces. They secured two old motor-car radiators and tinkered about with them until they had fashioned them into an aeroplane radiator. They soldered here, and brazed there, and tinkered there and worked magic until the Flying Wreck was herself again.

"As good as ever," declared Parer enthusiastically.

"Better," said McIntosh. "Hurrah!"

With a whoop and a yell and a laugh they took to the air again. She rose like a bird, a very noisy bird – but she flew to Penang. And the old engine konked out again.

"She's certainly a bit wheezy in the chest," said Parer, "but she's brought us here, all the same."

"A week or two will fix her up," declared McIntosh confidently. "We're sure to pick up some gadgets here and there."

They picked up the "gadgets" all right, but it meant three weeks' hard work before the Wreck was ready for the air once more.

Parer gave a grunt or satisfaction. "She's all ready for the air again," he said, as they stood off and surveyed their handiwork.

"Yes," answered McIntosh, "here's where we get corns on our rumpus again."

"She's certainly grown knobs in her lap," grinned Parer, "but we can't afford cushions."

They set out for Singapore over wonderful lands from which peeped cities where sunlight gleamed upon cupola and minaret. One day they zoomed over a jungle road and scared the life out of a herd of elephants and sent monkeys hysterically chattering over the tree-tops. But the old Wreck disapproved of their playfulness and came to earth in a paddyfield to the amazement of the Indian farmer. They patched her up again and just reached Singapore - the engine began to knonk out when they were just above that colourful city. They listened their hearts beating painfully. How often they had listened to their grand old engine konking out? But this wheeze sounded different. It was the wheeze of a dying man, the wheeze of a hard-battling man whose heart at last is konking out for good.

They landed, they stepped out of her, their faces serious for once.

Carefully, anxiously, they overhauled the old engine.

It had konked out for the last time. It would never fly again.

Not even the greatest machine shop in the world could have repaired this engine. It had worn out completely, just like a broken man's heart.

No money. No engine.

The kindly Dutch Government came to the rescue. Great sportsmen, the Dutch. They gave the adventurers a new engine.

But it took the two men two months' work to install the engine and recondition the Wreck ready for flying.

They rose above Singapore with a triumphant roar - and sped straight into a thunderstorm. Instantly the plane was spun around and only Parer's magic touch saved it from a last crash. Like a broken-winged duck she came hobbling back to Singapore - with a big hole blown through a wing. Great work that, to land the disabled plane without a crash.

They took off their coats and repaired her again - and flew to Gisee and crashed their fifth propeller and smashed the fuselage. They picked themselves out of the wreck.

"Corns on my rumpus, a lump on my head, a tooth sticking through my ear, and eyes all full of stars," sighed McIntosh. "Tell me Ray, am I coming or going.

"Wait until my head stops spinning," Parer answered, from "I'm seeing so many things and they're all chasing one another around and around in a whirling sky."

They patched her up again and in delight set off for Surabaya, magic city of the Dutch East Indies. They were nearing home. They took the air again on the last lap - the crossing of the Timor Sea. Never had the old Wreck flown so well, never had aeroplane engine hummed so sweetly for Oh! her nose was pointed towards Australia!

Far above the Spice Islands, set like emeralds upon a deep blue sea, they hummed out over the Timor and their hearts were singing with the engine. Darwin! Australia! Would they reach Darwin? At last. If the God of the Air only held their old plane together while crossing this last ocean, Australia's Timor Sea!

They did it. At 6.30 p.m. on 2 August, 206 days after leaving England, they landed at Darwin - with the petrol tanks bone dry!

Cheery Australians greeted them, pearlers and buffalo shooters, business men and police, cattlemen and men of the North, of Australia. And marvelled at their luck. Empty petrol tanks and the sea safely crossed behind them.

But they had their last accident, smashed the poor old nose of the Wreck. With a laugh they commandeered a sheet of galvanised iron and patched up the old nose that had weathered many a gale, survived many and many a hard bump. Then across their own Australian continent they flew with laughing hearts to journey's end.

And then! From the very heart of the Flying Wreck, wrapped around so very, very carefully it was, they reverently took out the little present sent by Lord Dewar.

"I wouldn't have damaged it for worlds," said Parer, giving it an affectionate pat. "Just think of all the crashes it has come through!"

McIntosh nodded. "Lord Dewar was so very good to us," he said. "I am so glad that we can deliver his present to his friend."

And they took off their old worn caps to the Flying Wreck.

Such, very shortly, is the story of the wonderful men, of a grand old plane and of a great flight half way across the then-uncharted sky of the world. When you visit Canberra go and touch your cap to the old Flying Wreck, safe in the Australian War Museum.

Poor McIntosh, alas, was killed a year later in a flying accident in Western Australia. Parer has since lived through very many air adventures. He was one of the grand pioneers of flying in New Guinea. And now, in yet another great war, he has donned flying uniform again.

While our Australia breeds such men as these our country can never die.

Ray Parer and John McIntosh with their Wreck, back in Australia.

ETT IMPRINT has the following ION IDRIESS books in print in 2025:

Prospecting for Gold (1931)
Lasseter's Last Ride (1931)
Flynn of the Inland (1932)
The Desert Column (1932)
Men of the Jungle (1932)
Drums of Mer (1933)
Gold-Dust and Ashes (1933)
The Yellow Joss (1934)
Man Tracks (1935)
Over the Range (1937)
Forty Fathoms Deep (1937)
Madman's Island (1938)
Headhunters of the Coral Sea (1940)
Lightning Ridge (1940)
Nemarluk (1941)
Shoot to Kill (1942)
Sniping (1942)
Guerrilla Tactics (1942)
Trapping the Jap (1942)
Lurking Death (1942)
The Scout (1943)
Horrie the Wog Dog (1945)
In Crocodile Land (1946)
The Opium Smugglers (1948)
The Wild White Man of Badu (1950)
Outlaws of the Leopolds (1952)
The Red Chief (1953)
The Silver City (1956)
Coral Sea Calling (1957)
Back O' Cairns (1958)
The Wild North (1960)
Tracks of Destiny (1961)
Gouger of the Bulletin (2013)
Ion Idriess: The Last Interview (2020)
Ion Idriess Letters (2023)
Walkabout (2024)